THE Shadow 1941

MARVEL GRAPHIC NOVEL

HITLER'S ASTROLOGER

Story: **Denny O'Neil And Michael Kaluta**
Pencils: **Michael Kaluta**
Inks: **Russ Heath**
Colors: **Mark Chiarello, Nick Jainschigg, John Wellington**
Letters: **Phil Felix**
Editor: **Larry Hama**
Managing Editor: **Pat Redding**
Editor in Chief: **Tom DeFalco**

Special thanks to:

Sky Books	Gateway Hobbies	Jeffery Ethell	Doug Murray
Portugese Tourist Board	Paul Fillingham	Jerry Shattenburg	Joel Gross

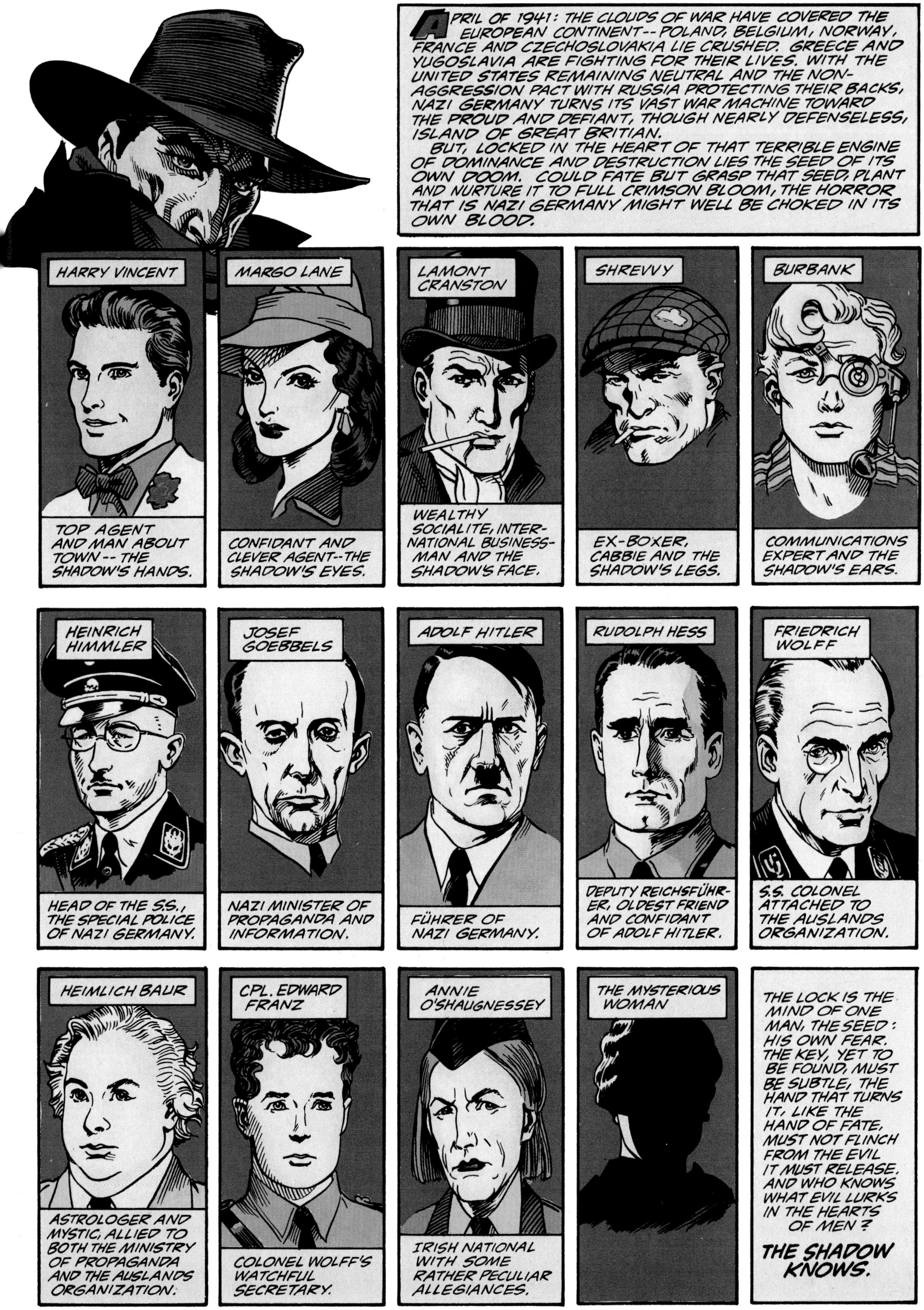
APRIL OF 1941: THE CLOUDS OF WAR HAVE COVERED THE EUROPEAN CONTINENT-- POLAND, BELGIUM, NORWAY, FRANCE AND CZECHOSLOVAKIA LIE CRUSHED. GREECE AND YUGOSLAVIA ARE FIGHTING FOR THEIR LIVES. WITH THE UNITED STATES REMAINING NEUTRAL AND THE NON-AGGRESSION PACT WITH RUSSIA PROTECTING THEIR BACKS, NAZI GERMANY TURNS ITS VAST WAR MACHINE TOWARD THE PROUD AND DEFIANT, THOUGH NEARLY DEFENSELESS, ISLAND OF GREAT BRITIAN.
BUT, LOCKED IN THE HEART OF THAT TERRIBLE ENGINE OF DOMINANCE AND DESTRUCTION LIES THE SEED OF ITS OWN DOOM. COULD FATE BUT GRASP THAT SEED, PLANT AND NURTURE IT TO FULL CRIMSON BLOOM, THE HORROR THAT IS NAZI GERMANY MIGHT WELL BE CHOKED IN ITS OWN BLOOD.
HARRY VINCENT
TOP AGENT AND MAN ABOUT TOWN -- THE SHADOW'S HANDS.
MARGO LANE
CONFIDANT AND CLEVER AGENT--THE SHADOW'S EYES.
LAMONT CRANSTON
WEALTHY SOCIALITE, INTERNATIONAL BUSINESSMAN AND THE SHADOW'S FACE.
SHREVVY
EX-BOXER, CABBIE AND THE SHADOW'S LEGS.
BURBANK
COMMUNICATIONS EXPERT AND THE SHADOW'S EARS.
HEINRICH HIMMLER
HEAD OF THE S.S., THE SPECIAL POLICE OF NAZI GERMANY.
JOSEF GOEBBELS
NAZI MINISTER OF PROPAGANDA AND INFORMATION.
ADOLF HITLER
FÜHRER OF NAZI GERMANY.
RUDOLPH HESS
DEPUTY REICHSFÜHRER, OLDEST FRIEND AND CONFIDANT OF ADOLF HITLER.
FRIEDRICH WOLFF
S.S. COLONEL ATTACHED TO THE AUSLANDS ORGANIZATION.
HEIMLICH BAUR
ASTROLOGER AND MYSTIC, ALLIED TO BOTH THE MINISTRY OF PROPAGANDA AND THE AUSLANDS ORGANIZATION.
CPL. EDWARD FRANZ
COLONEL WOLFF'S WATCHFUL SECRETARY.
ANNIE O'SHAUGNESSEY
IRISH NATIONAL WITH SOME RATHER PECULIAR ALLEGIANCES.
THE MYSTERIOUS WOMAN
THE LOCK IS THE MIND OF ONE MAN, THE SEED: HIS OWN FEAR. THE KEY, YET TO BE FOUND, MUST BE SUBTLE, THE HAND THAT TURNS IT, LIKE THE HAND OF FATE, MUST NOT FLINCH FROM THE EVIL IT MUST RELEASE. AND WHO KNOWS WHAT EVIL LURKS IN THE HEARTS OF MEN?
THE SHADOW KNOWS.

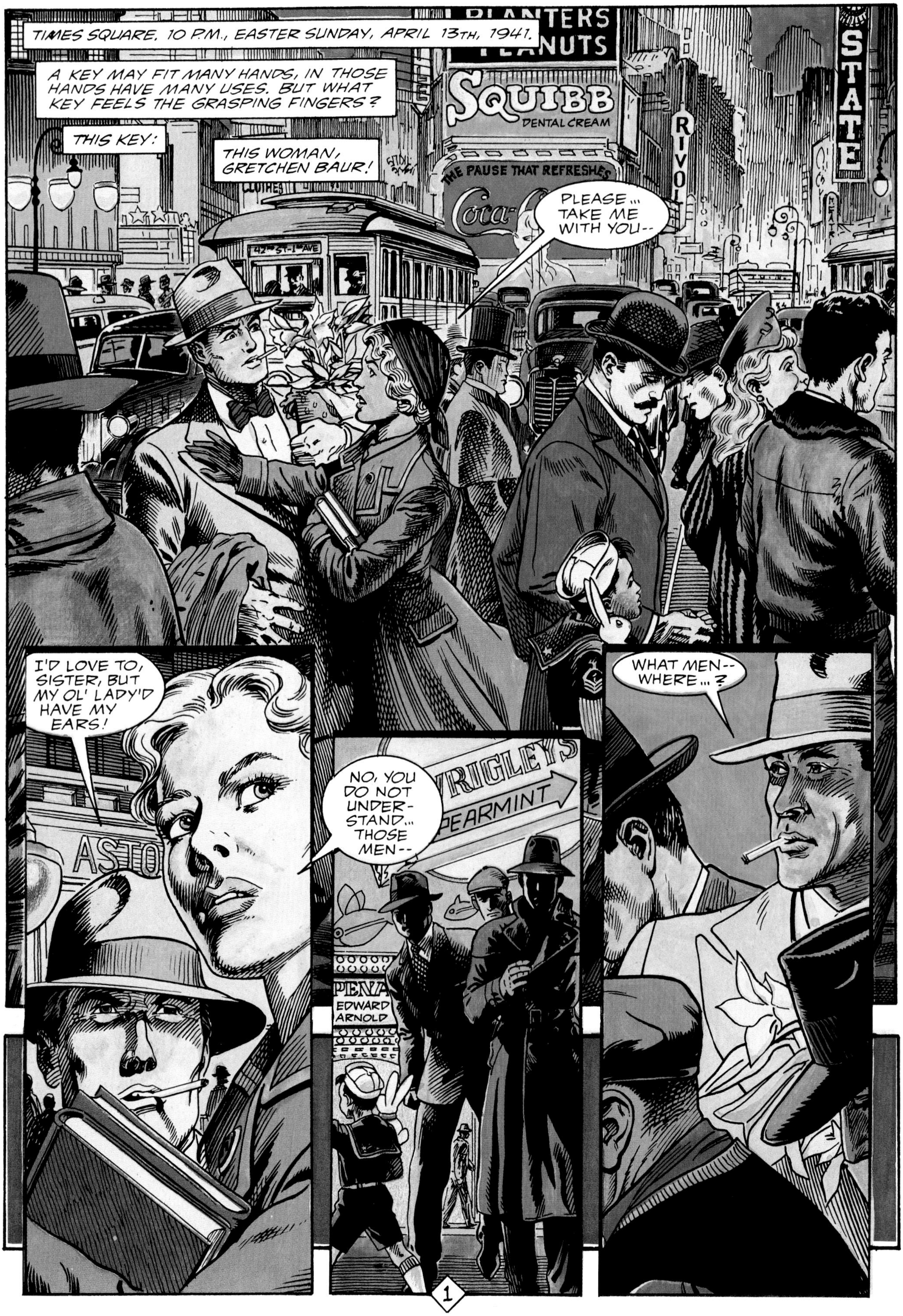
TIMES SQUARE, 10 P.M., EASTER SUNDAY, APRIL 13TH, 1941.
A KEY MAY FIT MANY HANDS, IN THOSE HANDS HAVE MANY USES. BUT WHAT KEY FEELS THE GRASPING FINGERS?
THIS KEY:
THIS WOMAN, GRETCHEN BAUR!
PLEASE... TAKE ME WITH YOU--
I'D LOVE TO, SISTER, BUT MY OL' LADY'D HAVE MY EARS!
NO, YOU DO NOT UNDERSTAND... THOSE MEN--
WHAT MEN-- WHERE...?
SQUIBB
DENTAL CREAM
THE PAUSE THAT REFRESHES
STATE
EDWARD
ARNOLD

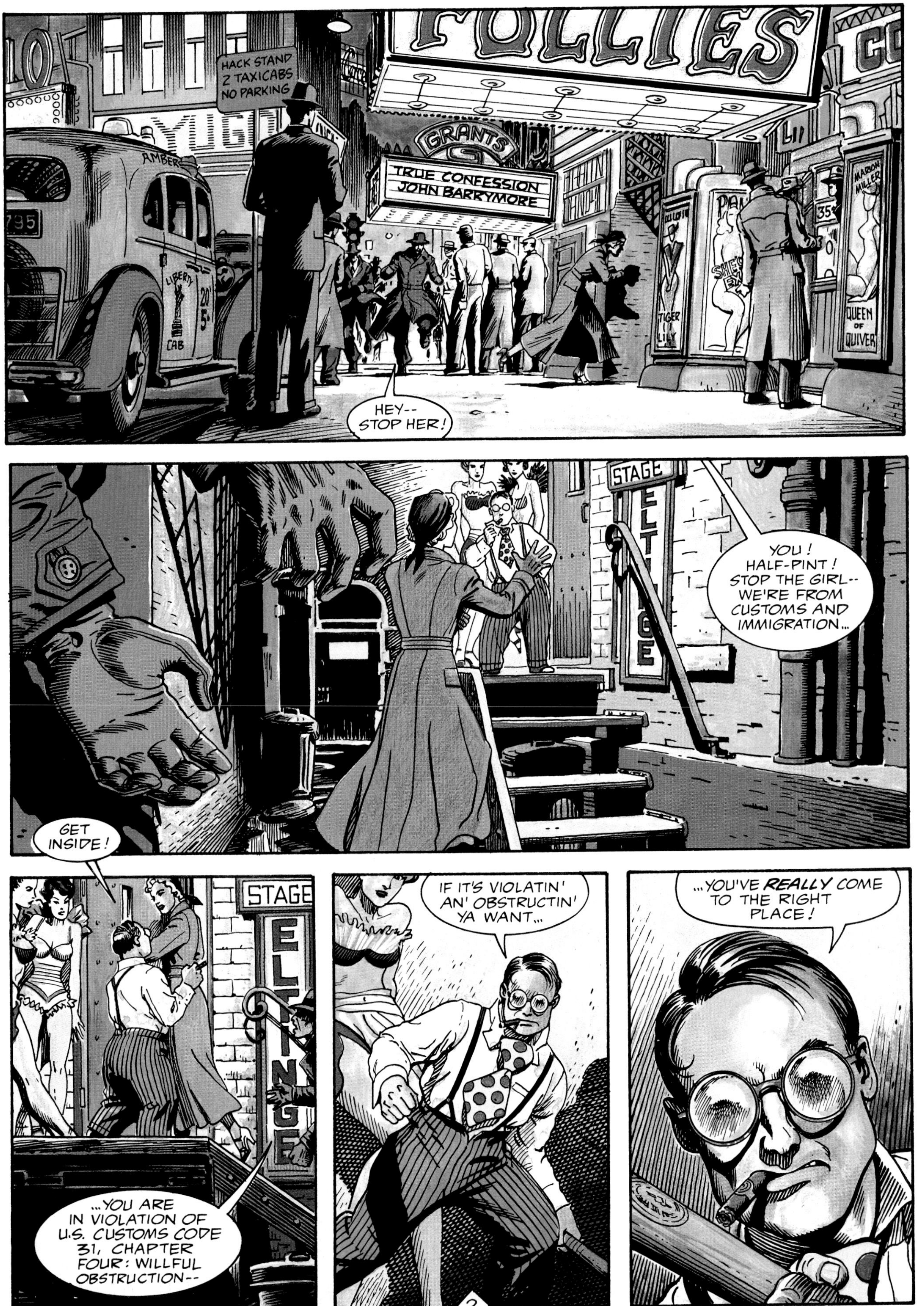
FOLLIES
HACK STAND
2 TAXICABS
NO PARKING
GRANTS
TRUE CONFESSION
JOHN BARRYMORE
LIBERTY CAB
TIGER LILY
MARION MILLER
QUEEN OF QUIVER
HEY-- STOP HER!
STAGE
ELTINGE
YOU! HALF-PINT! STOP THE GIRL-- WE'RE FROM CUSTOMS AND IMMIGRATION...
GET INSIDE!
...YOU ARE IN VIOLATION OF U.S. CUSTOMS CODE 31, CHAPTER FOUR: WILLFUL OBSTRUCTION--
IF IT'S VIOLATIN' AN' OBSTRUCTIN' YA WANT...
...YOU'VE *REALLY* COME TO THE RIGHT PLACE!

WOULD YOU LIKE TO TASTE MY MILK, SIR?

YOU BET! 'N THEN I'D LIKE TO FILL YER BUCKETS!

NIX, NIX! AMSCRAY, BRAT!

OKAY, DOLL, FUN'S OVER...

HEY BAYBEE! TAKE IT OFF!

YER COMIN' WID US!

I'M AFRAID NOT, FRITZIE.

MISS BAUR, IF I MAY SUGGEST...?

...IF ANYONE HAD HIS HAND OVER MY MOUTH, I'D BITE HIM SO HARD--

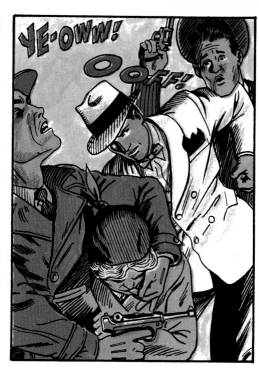

YE-OWW!

OOFF!

3

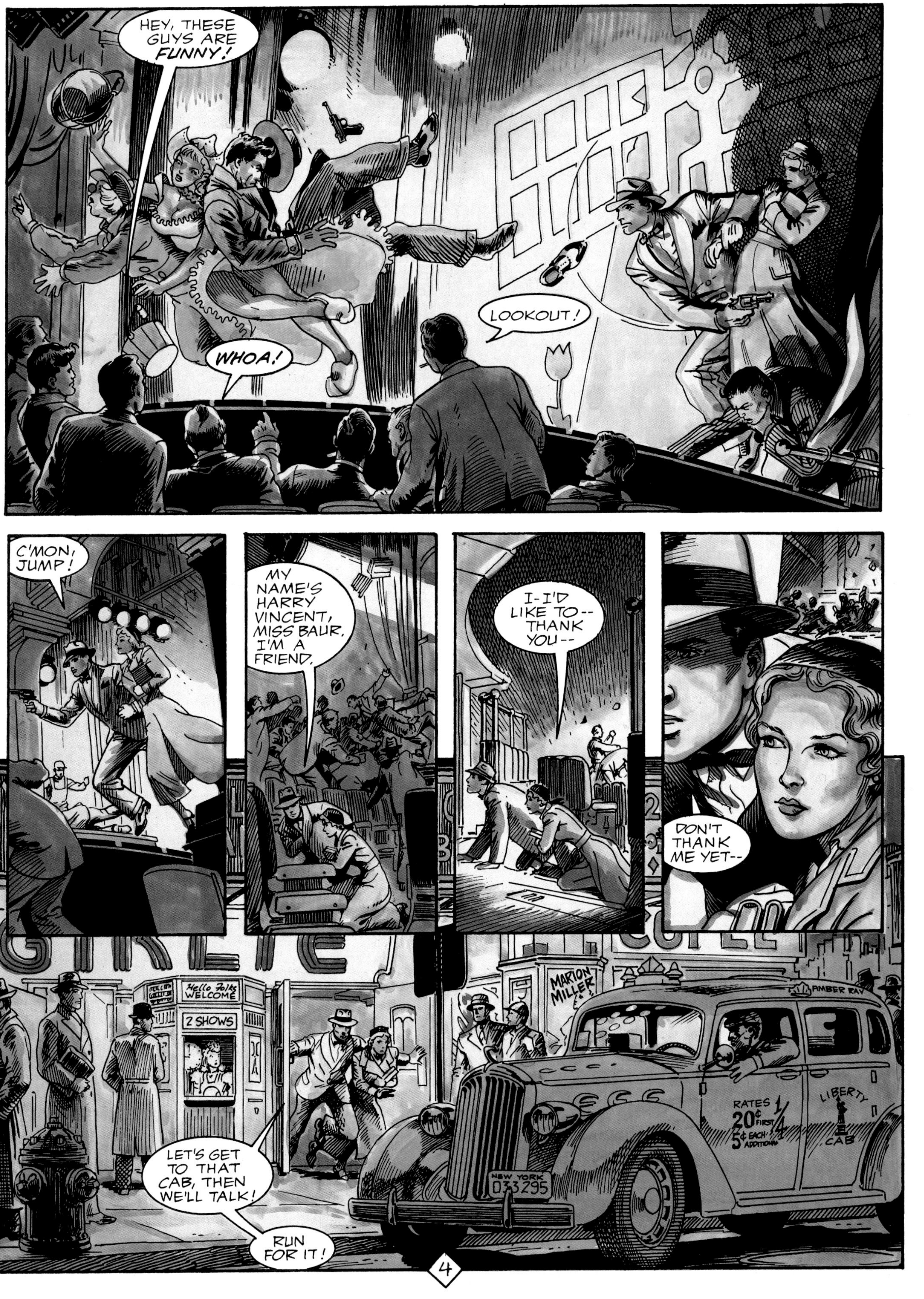
HEY, THESE GUYS ARE FUNNY!
WHOA!
LOOKOUT!
C'MON, JUMP!
MY NAME'S HARRY VINCENT, MISS BAUR, I'M A FRIEND.
I-I'D LIKE TO-- THANK YOU--
DON'T THANK ME YET--
Hello Folks WELCOME
2 SHOWS
MARION MILLER
AMBER RAY
RATES 20¢ FIRST 1/4 5¢ EACH ADDITIONAL 1/4
LIBERTY CAB
NEW YORK D33295
LET'S GET TO THAT CAB, THEN WE'LL TALK!
RUN FOR IT!

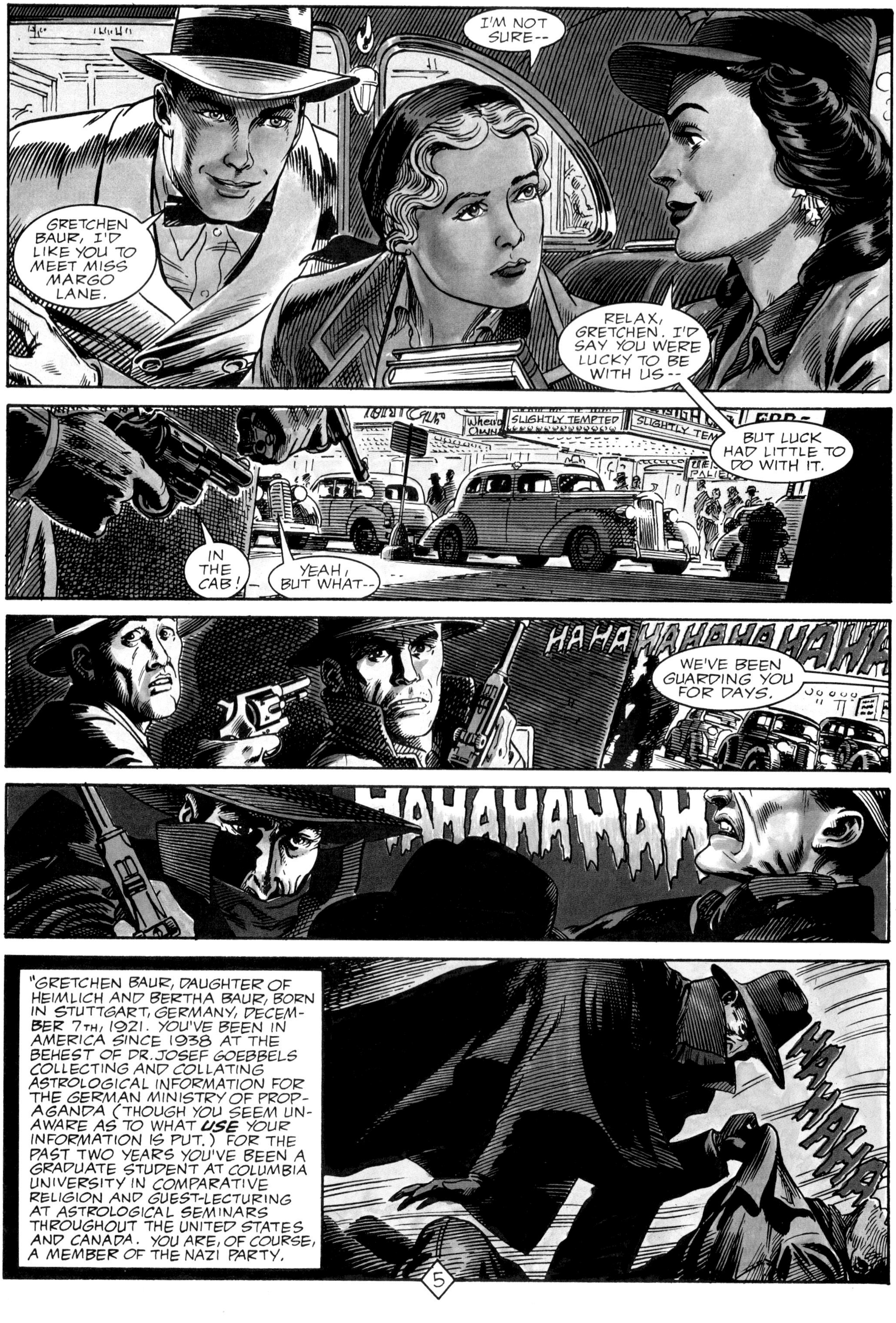
I'M NOT SURE--
GRETCHEN BAUR, I'D LIKE YOU TO MEET MISS MARGO LANE.
RELAX, GRETCHEN. I'D SAY YOU WERE LUCKY TO BE WITH US--
SLIGHTLY TEMPTED
BUT LUCK HAD LITTLE TO DO WITH IT.
IN THE CAB!
YEAH, BUT WHAT--
HA HA HAHAHAHAHAHA
WE'VE BEEN GUARDING YOU FOR DAYS.
HAHAHAHAHAH
"GRETCHEN BAUR, DAUGHTER OF HEIMLICH AND BERTHA BAUR, BORN IN STUTTGART, GERMANY, DECEMBER 7TH, 1921. YOU'VE BEEN IN AMERICA SINCE 1938 AT THE BEHEST OF DR. JOSEF GOEBBELS COLLECTING AND COLLATING ASTROLOGICAL INFORMATION FOR THE GERMAN MINISTRY OF PROPAGANDA (THOUGH YOU SEEM UNAWARE AS TO WHAT ***USE*** YOUR INFORMATION IS PUT.) FOR THE PAST TWO YEARS YOU'VE BEEN A GRADUATE STUDENT AT COLUMBIA UNIVERSITY IN COMPARATIVE RELIGION AND GUEST-LECTURING AT ASTROLOGICAL SEMINARS THROUGHOUT THE UNITED STATES AND CANADA. YOU ARE, OF COURSE, A MEMBER OF THE NAZI PARTY.
HAHAHAHA

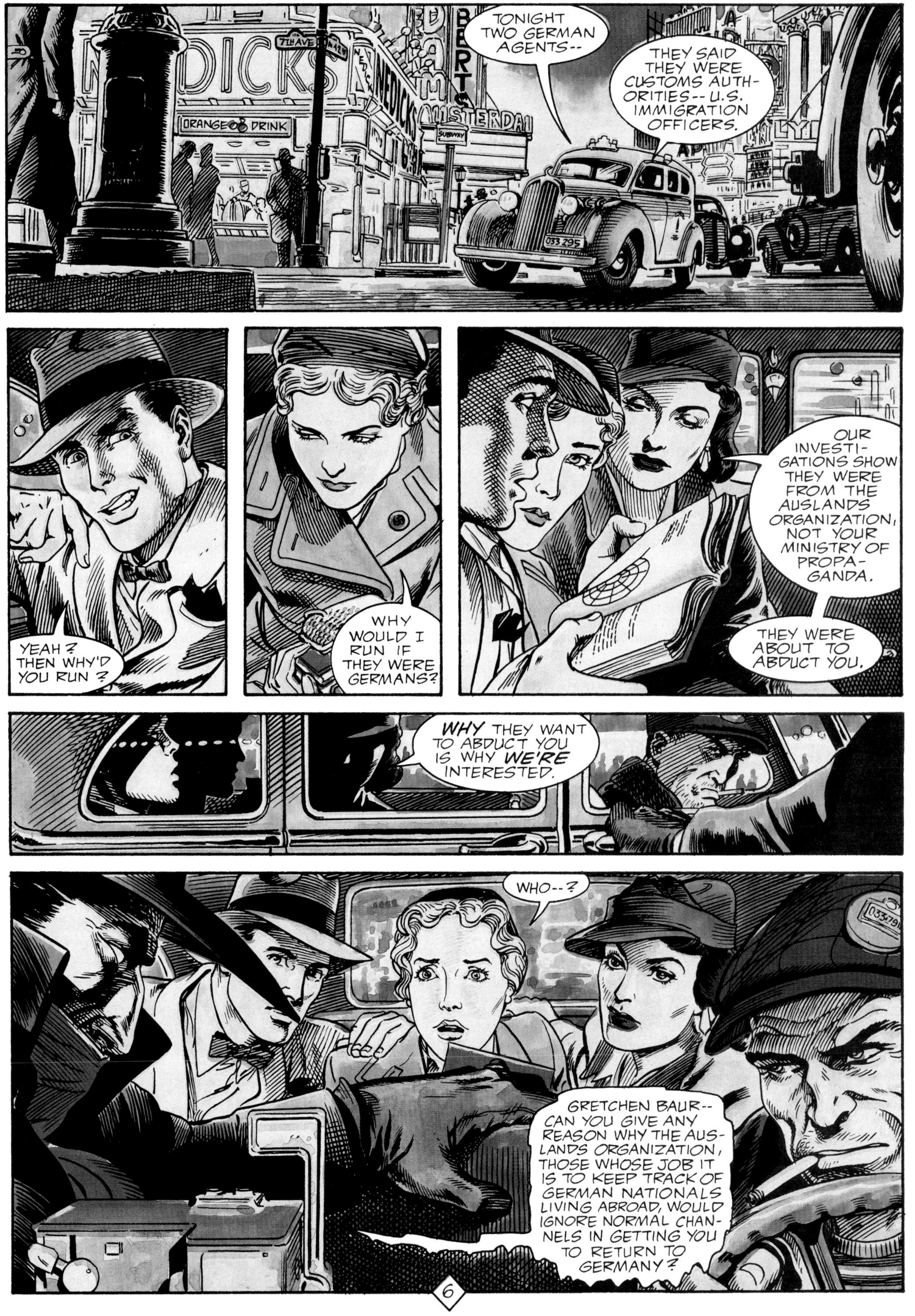
7th AVE
NEDICKS
ORANGE DRINK
SUBWAY
TONIGHT TWO GERMAN AGENTS--
THEY SAID THEY WERE CUSTOMS AUTH-ORITIES--U.S. IMMIGRATION OFFICERS.
YEAH? THEN WHY'D YOU RUN?
WHY WOULD I RUN IF THEY WERE GERMANS?
OUR INVESTI-GATIONS SHOW THEY WERE FROM THE AUSLANDS ORGANIZATION, NOT YOUR MINISTRY OF PROPA-GANDA.
THEY WERE ABOUT TO ABDUCT YOU.
WHY THEY WANT TO ABDUCT YOU IS WHY WE'RE INTERESTED.
WHO--?
GRETCHEN BAUR-- CAN YOU GIVE ANY REASON WHY THE AUS-LANDS ORGANIZATION, THOSE WHOSE JOB IT IS TO KEEP TRACK OF GERMAN NATIONALS LIVING ABROAD, WOULD IGNORE NORMAL CHAN-NELS IN GETTING YOU TO RETURN TO GERMANY?

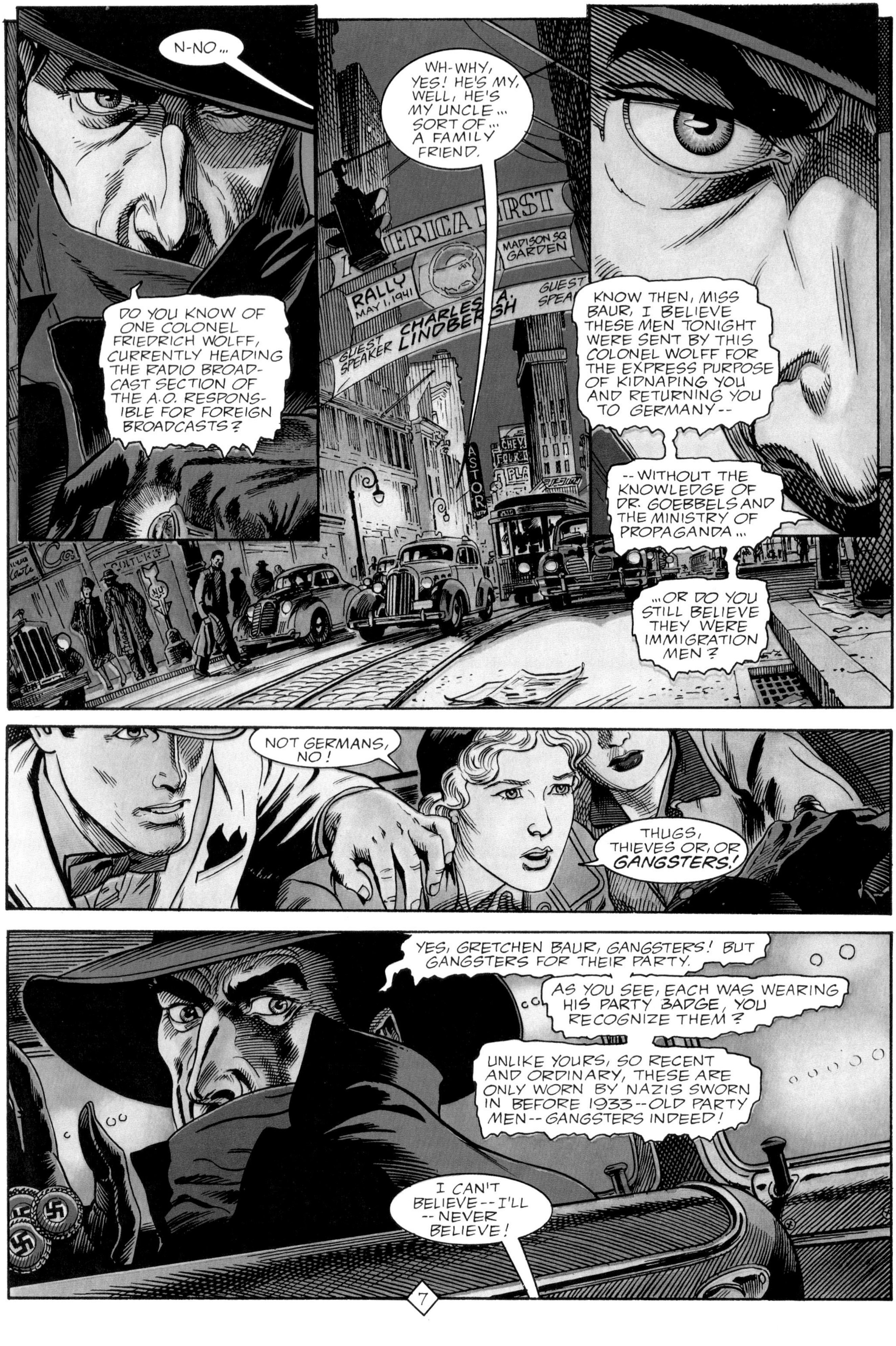
N-NO...
WH-WHY, YES! HE'S MY, WELL, HE'S MY UNCLE... SORT OF... A FAMILY FRIEND.
AMERICA FIRST
MADISON SQ GARDEN
RALLY MAY 1, 1941
GUEST SPEAKER CHARLES A. LINDBERGH
DO YOU KNOW OF ONE COLONEL FRIEDRICH WOLFF, CURRENTLY HEADING THE RADIO BROAD-CAST SECTION OF THE A.O. RESPONS-IBLE FOR FOREIGN BROADCASTS?
ASTOR
KNOW THEN, MISS BAUR, I BELIEVE THESE MEN TONIGHT WERE SENT BY THIS COLONEL WOLFF FOR THE EXPRESS PURPOSE OF KIDNAPING YOU AND RETURNING YOU TO GERMANY--
--WITHOUT THE KNOWLEDGE OF DR. GOEBBELS AND THE MINISTRY OF PROPAGANDA...
...OR DO YOU STILL BELIEVE THEY WERE IMMIGRATION MEN?
NOT GERMANS, NO!
THUGS, THIEVES OR, OR GANGSTERS!
YES, GRETCHEN BAUR, GANGSTERS! BUT GANGSTERS FOR THEIR PARTY.
AS YOU SEE, EACH WAS WEARING HIS PARTY BADGE, YOU RECOGNIZE THEM?
UNLIKE YOURS, SO RECENT AND ORDINARY, THESE ARE ONLY WORN BY NAZIS SWORN IN BEFORE 1933--OLD PARTY MEN--GANGSTERS INDEED!
I CAN'T BELIEVE--I'LL--NEVER BELIEVE!

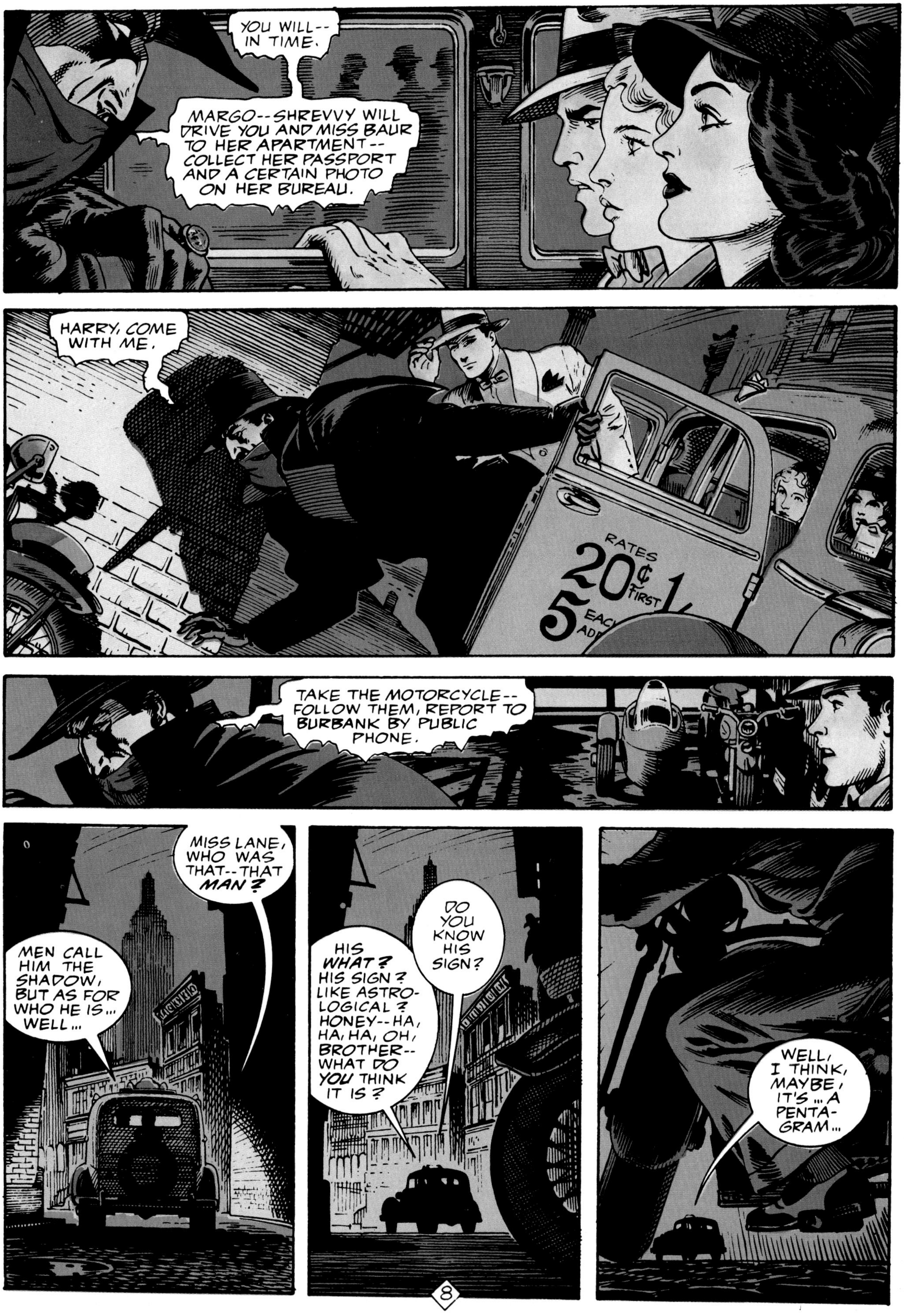
YOU WILL-- IN TIME.
MARGO--SHREVVY WILL DRIVE YOU AND MISS BAUR TO HER APARTMENT-- COLLECT HER PASSPORT AND A CERTAIN PHOTO ON HER BUREAU.
HARRY, COME WITH ME.
RATES 20¢ FIRST
TAKE THE MOTORCYCLE-- FOLLOW THEM, REPORT TO BURBANK BY PUBLIC PHONE.
MISS LANE, WHO WAS THAT--THAT MAN?
MEN CALL HIM THE SHADOW, BUT AS FOR WHO HE IS... WELL...
DO YOU KNOW HIS SIGN?
HIS WHAT? HIS SIGN? LIKE ASTROLOGICAL? HONEY--HA, HA, HA, OH, BROTHER-- WHAT DO YOU THINK IT IS?
WELL, I THINK, MAYBE, IT'S... A PENTAGRAM...

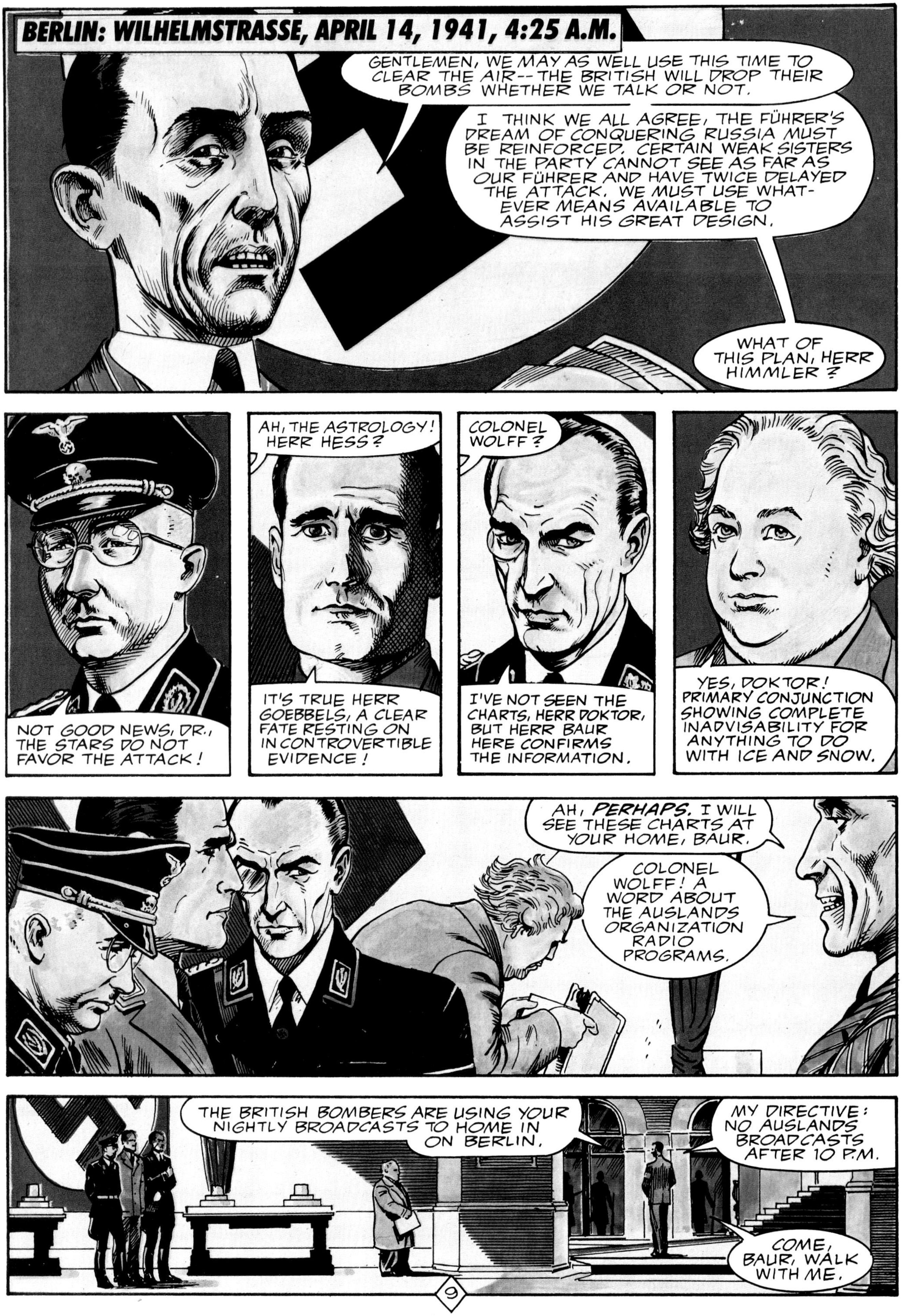
BERLIN: WILHELMSTRASSE, APRIL 14, 1941, 4:25 A.M.
GENTLEMEN, WE MAY AS WELL USE THIS TIME TO CLEAR THE AIR-- THE BRITISH WILL DROP THEIR BOMBS WHETHER WE TALK OR NOT.
I THINK WE ALL AGREE, THE FÜHRER'S DREAM OF CONQUERING RUSSIA MUST BE REINFORCED. CERTAIN WEAK SISTERS IN THE PARTY CANNOT SEE AS FAR AS OUR FÜHRER AND HAVE TWICE DELAYED THE ATTACK. WE MUST USE WHAT-EVER MEANS AVAILABLE TO ASSIST HIS GREAT DESIGN.
WHAT OF THIS PLAN, HERR HIMMLER?
NOT GOOD NEWS, DR., THE STARS DO NOT FAVOR THE ATTACK!
AH, THE ASTROLOGY! HERR HESS?
IT'S TRUE HERR GOEBBELS, A CLEAR FATE RESTING ON INCONTROVERTIBLE EVIDENCE!
COLONEL WOLFF?
I'VE NOT SEEN THE CHARTS, HERR DOKTOR, BUT HERR BAUR HERE CONFIRMS THE INFORMATION.
YES, DOKTOR! PRIMARY CONJUNCTION SHOWING COMPLETE INADVISABILITY FOR ANYTHING TO DO WITH ICE AND SNOW.
AH, PERHAPS. I WILL SEE THESE CHARTS AT YOUR HOME, BAUR.
COLONEL WOLFF! A WORD ABOUT THE AUSLANDS ORGANIZATION RADIO PROGRAMS.
THE BRITISH BOMBERS ARE USING YOUR NIGHTLY BROADCASTS TO HOME IN ON BERLIN.
MY DIRECTIVE: NO AUSLANDS BROADCASTS AFTER 10 P.M.
COME, BAUR, WALK WITH ME.

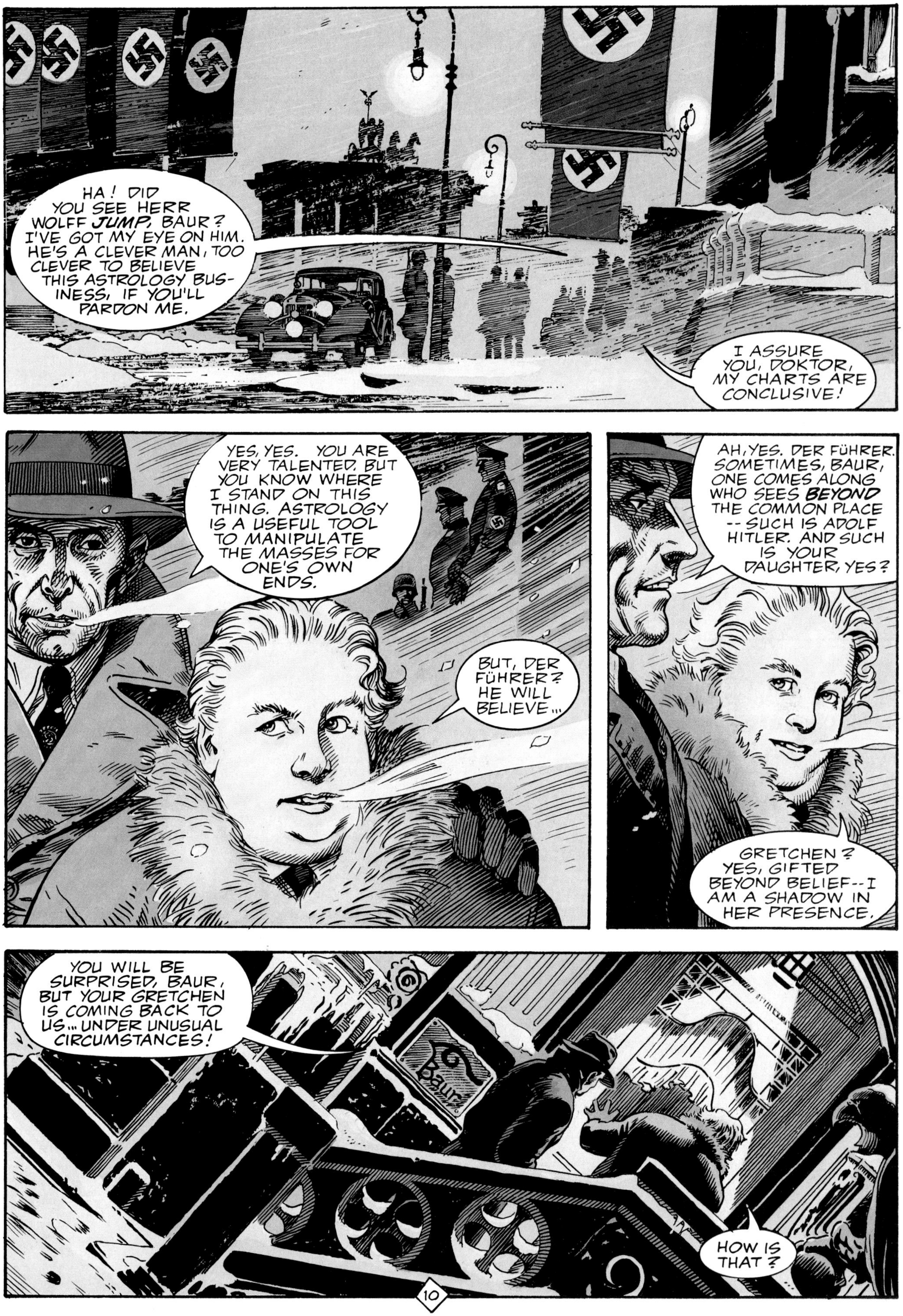
HA! DID YOU SEE HERR WOLFF JUMP, BAUR? I'VE GOT MY EYE ON HIM. HE'S A CLEVER MAN, TOO CLEVER TO BELIEVE THIS ASTROLOGY BUSINESS, IF YOU'LL PARDON ME.
I ASSURE YOU, DOKTOR, MY CHARTS ARE CONCLUSIVE!
YES, YES. YOU ARE VERY TALENTED, BUT YOU KNOW WHERE I STAND ON THIS THING. ASTROLOGY IS A USEFUL TOOL TO MANIPULATE THE MASSES FOR ONE'S OWN ENDS.
BUT, DER FÜHRER? HE WILL BELIEVE...
AH, YES. DER FÜHRER. SOMETIMES, BAUR, ONE COMES ALONG WHO SEES BEYOND THE COMMON PLACE -- SUCH IS ADOLF HITLER. AND SUCH IS YOUR DAUGHTER, YES?
GRETCHEN? YES, GIFTED BEYOND BELIEF--I AM A SHADOW IN HER PRESENCE.
YOU WILL BE SURPRISED, BAUR, BUT YOUR GRETCHEN IS COMING BACK TO US... UNDER UNUSUAL CIRCUMSTANCES!
Baur
HOW IS THAT?

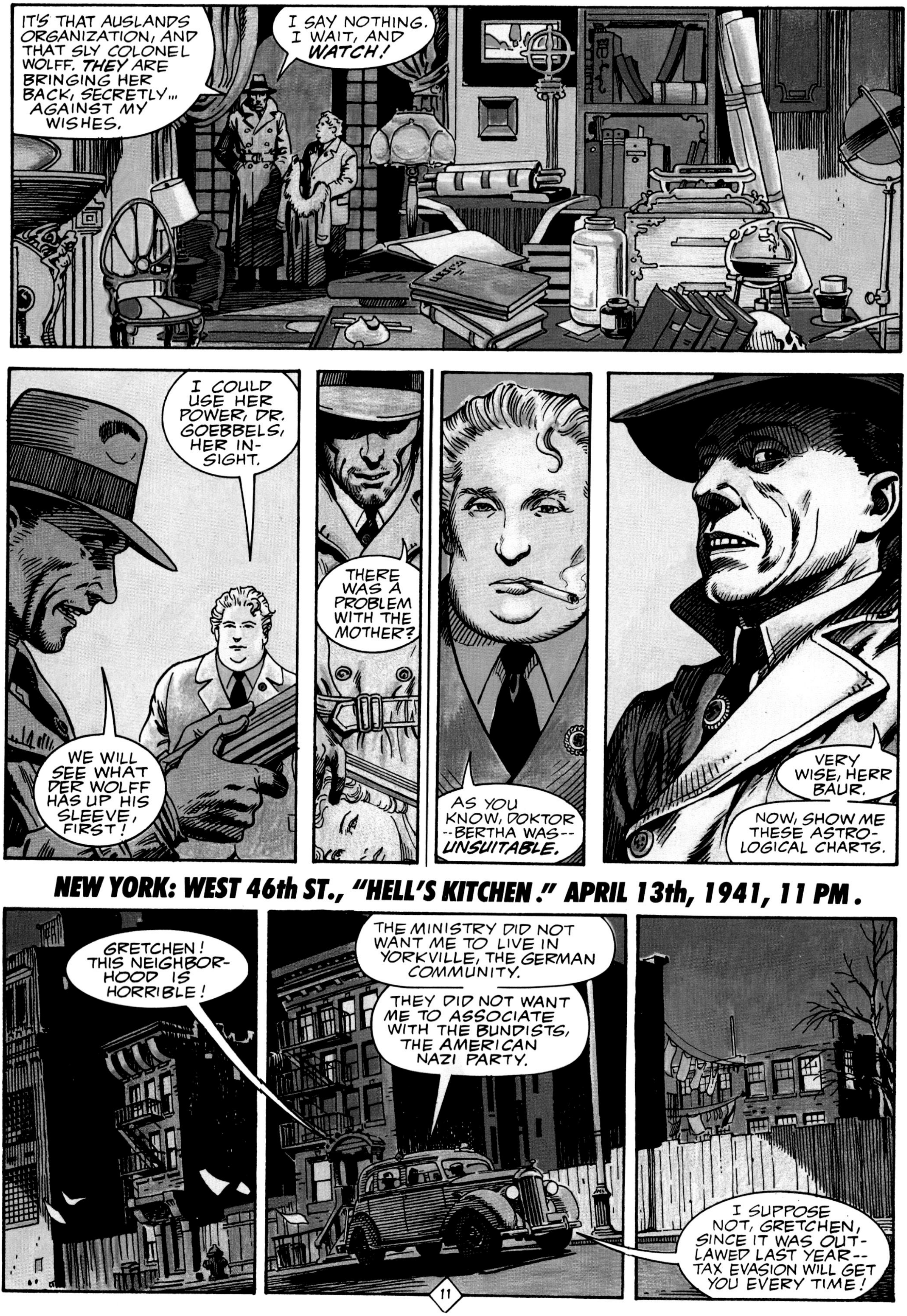
IT'S THAT AUSLANDS ORGANIZATION, AND THAT SLY COLONEL WOLFF. THEY ARE BRINGING HER BACK, SECRETLY... AGAINST MY WISHES.
I SAY NOTHING. I WAIT, AND WATCH!
I COULD USE HER POWER, DR. GOEBBELS, HER IN-SIGHT.
WE WILL SEE WHAT DER WOLFF HAS UP HIS SLEEVE, FIRST!
THERE WAS A PROBLEM WITH THE MOTHER?
AS YOU KNOW, DOKTOR --BERTHA WAS-- UNSUITABLE.
VERY WISE, HERR BAUR.
NOW, SHOW ME THESE ASTRO-LOGICAL CHARTS.
NEW YORK: WEST 46th ST., "HELL'S KITCHEN." APRIL 13th, 1941, 11 PM.
GRETCHEN! THIS NEIGHBOR-HOOD IS HORRIBLE!
THE MINISTRY DID NOT WANT ME TO LIVE IN YORKVILLE, THE GERMAN COMMUNITY.
THEY DID NOT WANT ME TO ASSOCIATE WITH THE BUNDISTS, THE AMERICAN NAZI PARTY.
I SUPPOSE NOT, GRETCHEN, SINCE IT WAS OUT-LAWED LAST YEAR-- TAX EVASION WILL GET YOU EVERY TIME!

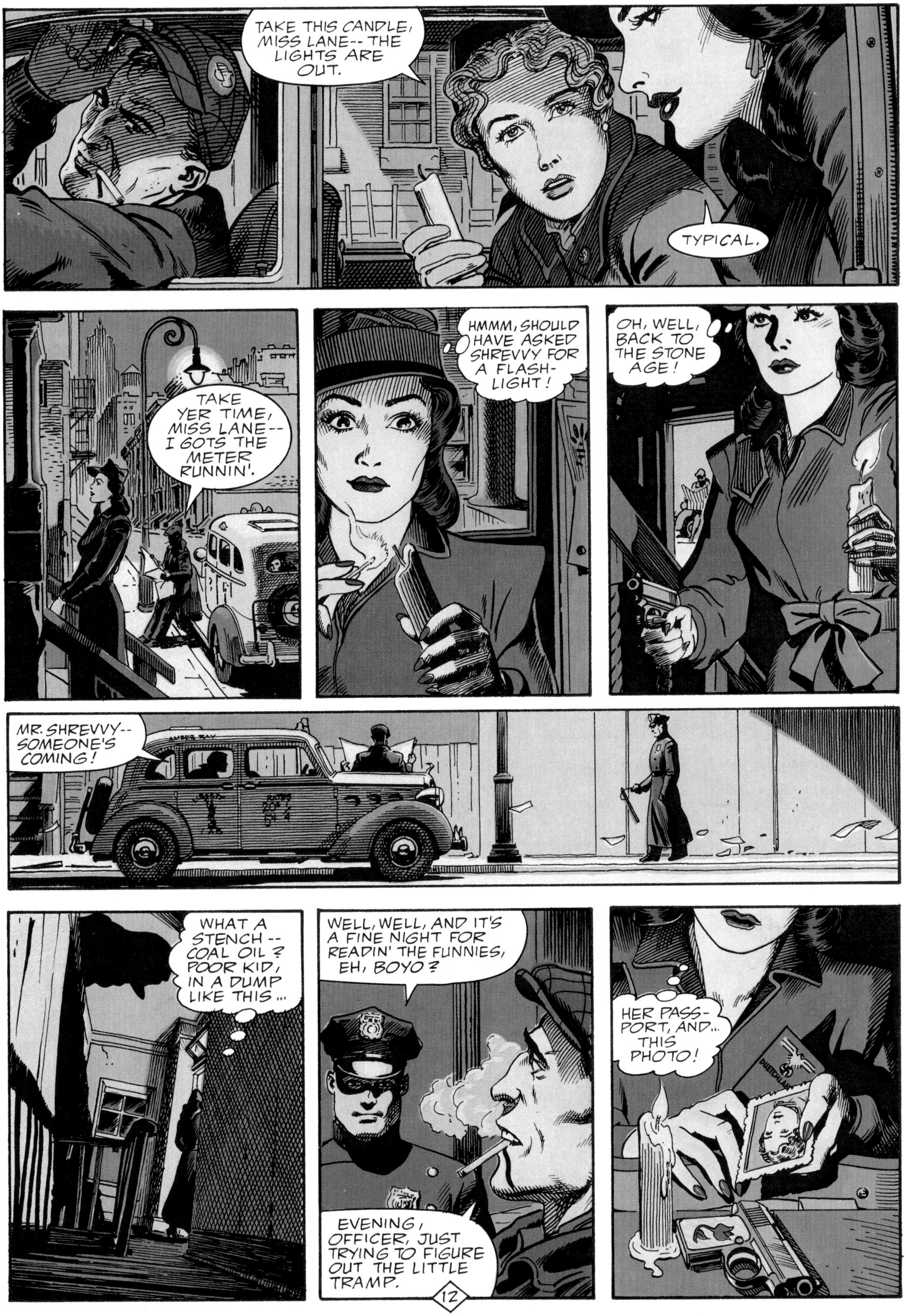
TAKE THIS CANDLE, MISS LANE-- THE LIGHTS ARE OUT.
TYPICAL.
TAKE YER TIME, MISS LANE-- I GOTS THE METER RUNNIN'.
HMMM, SHOULD HAVE ASKED SHREVVY FOR A FLASH-LIGHT!
OH, WELL, BACK TO THE STONE AGE!
MR. SHREVVY-- SOMEONE'S COMING!
WHAT A STENCH -- COAL OIL? POOR KID, IN A DUMP LIKE THIS...
WELL, WELL, AND IT'S A FINE NIGHT FOR READIN' THE FUNNIES, EH, BOYO?
EVENING, OFFICER, JUST TRYING TO FIGURE OUT THE LITTLE TRAMP.
HER PASS-PORT, AND... THIS PHOTO!

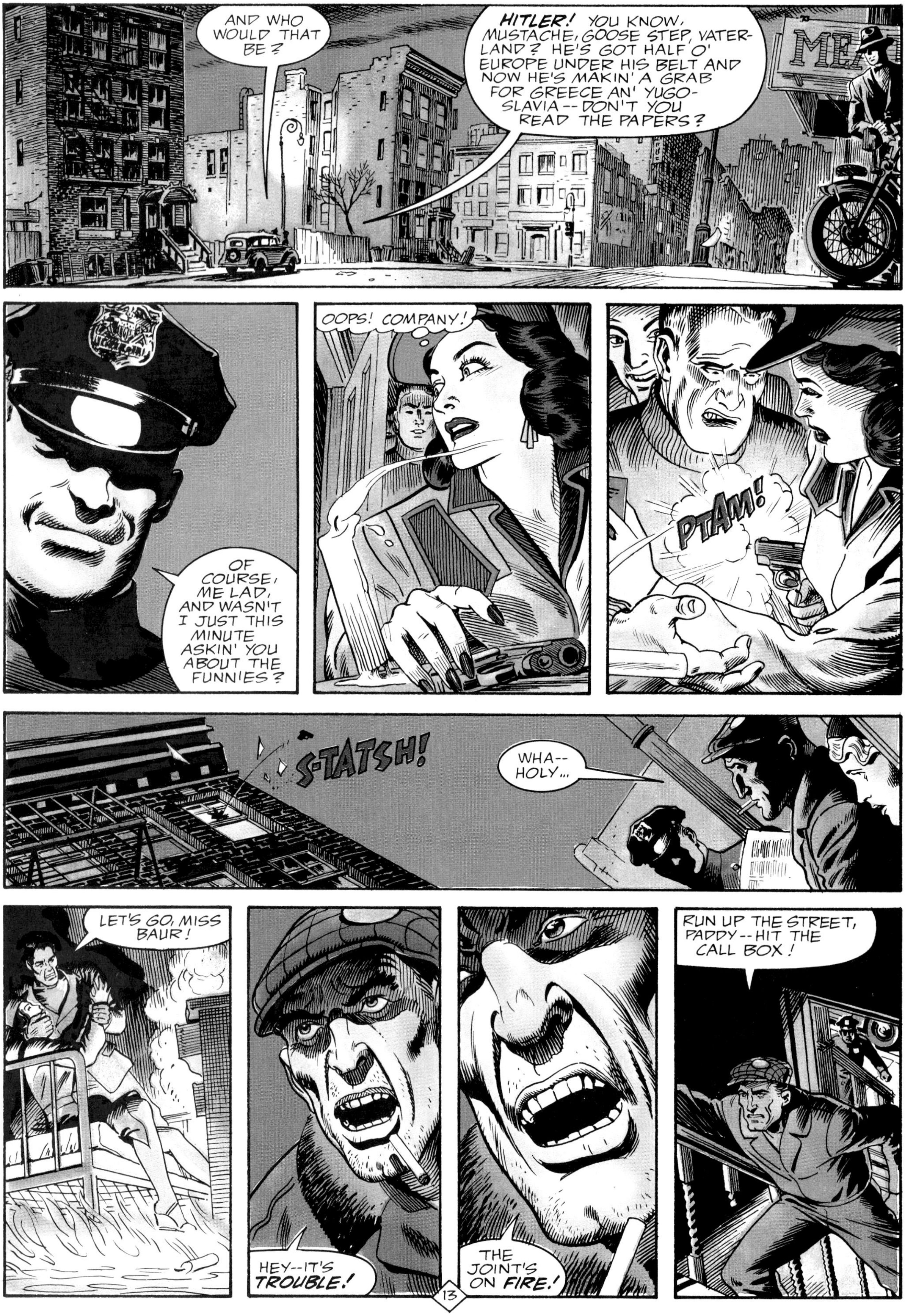
AND WHO WOULD THAT BE?
HITLER! YOU KNOW, MUSTACHE, GOOSE STEP, VATERLAND? HE'S GOT HALF O' EUROPE UNDER HIS BELT AND NOW HE'S MAKIN' A GRAB FOR GREECE AN' YUGOSLAVIA--DON'T YOU READ THE PAPERS?
OF COURSE, ME LAD, AND WASN'T I JUST THIS MINUTE ASKIN' YOU ABOUT THE FUNNIES?
OOPS! COMPANY!
PTAM!
S-TATSH!
WHA-- HOLY...
LET'S GO, MISS BAUR!
HEY--IT'S TROUBLE!
THE JOINT'S ON FIRE!
RUN UP THE STREET, PADDY--HIT THE CALL BOX!

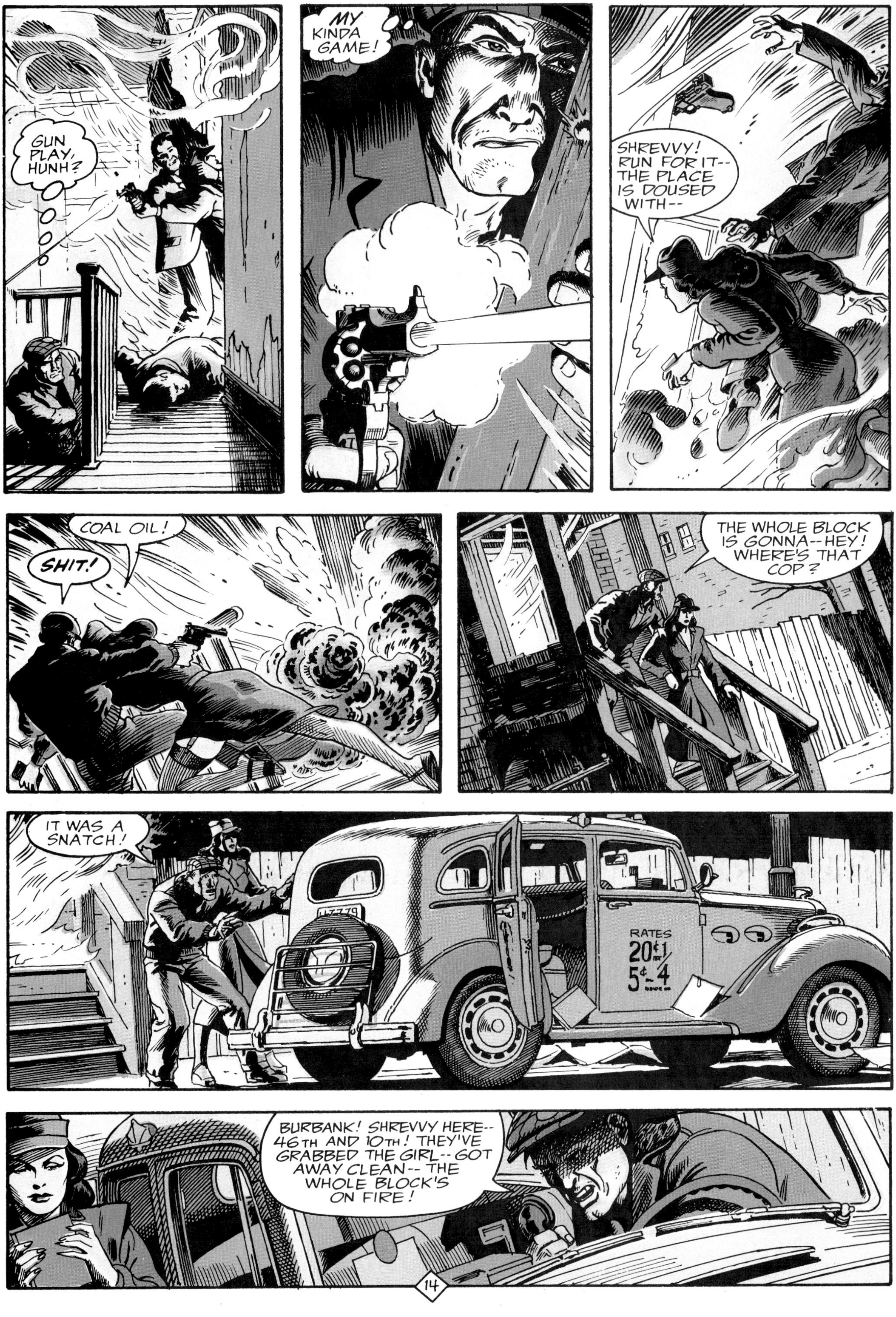
GUN PLAY, HUNH?
MY KINDA GAME!
SHREVVY! RUN FOR IT-- THE PLACE IS DOUSED WITH--
COAL OIL!
SHIT!
THE WHOLE BLOCK IS GONNA--HEY! WHERE'S THAT COP?
IT WAS A SNATCH!
RATES 20¢ 1ST 1/4 5¢ -- 1/4
BURBANK! SHREVVY HERE-- 46TH AND 10TH! THEY'VE GRABBED THE GIRL--GOT AWAY CLEAN-- THE WHOLE BLOCK'S ON FIRE!

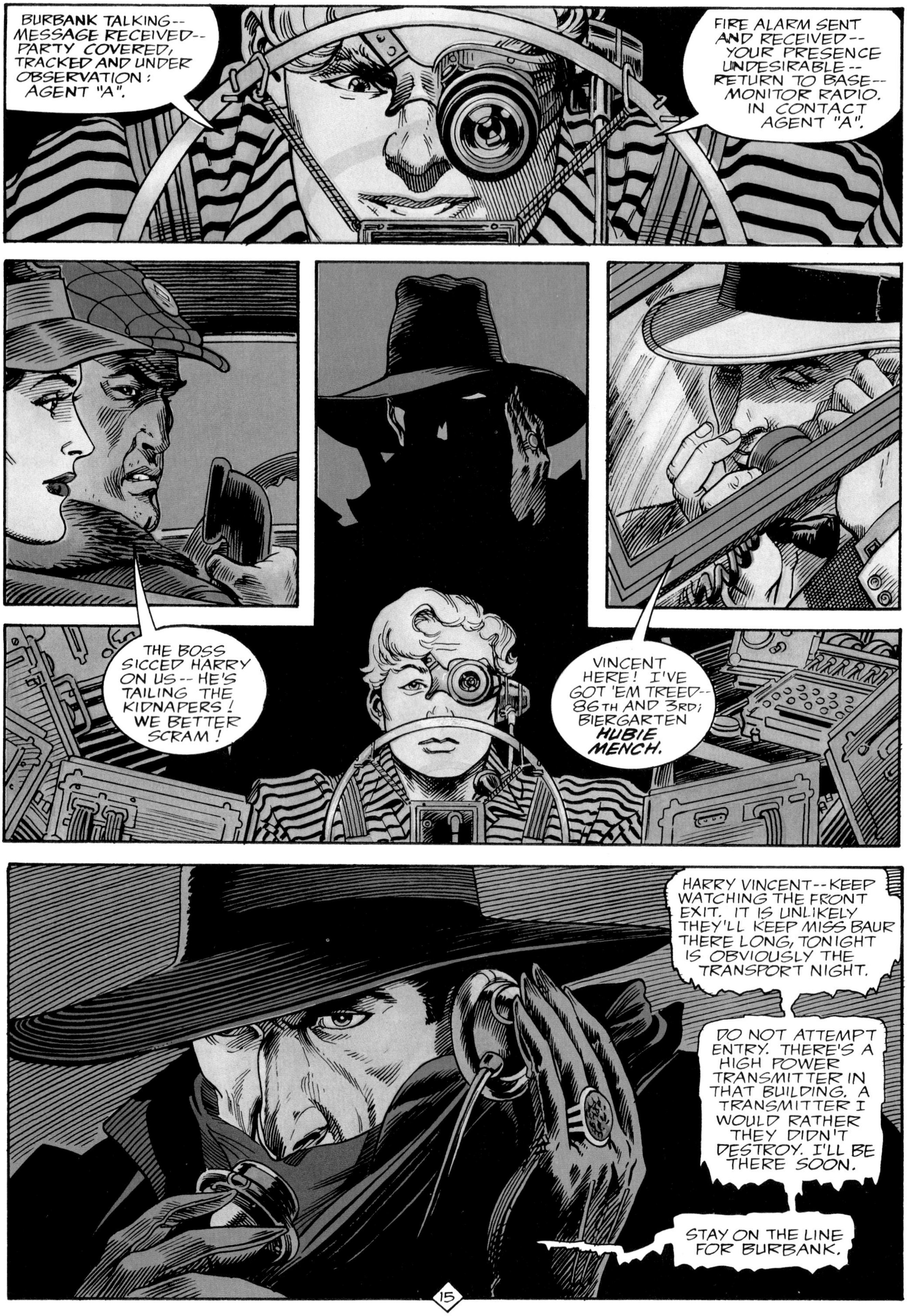
BURBANK TALKING--MESSAGE RECEIVED--PARTY COVERED, TRACKED AND UNDER OBSERVATION: AGENT "A".
FIRE ALARM SENT AND RECEIVED--YOUR PRESENCE UNDESIRABLE--RETURN TO BASE--MONITOR RADIO. IN CONTACT AGENT "A".
THE BOSS SICCED HARRY ON US--HE'S TAILING THE KIDNAPERS! WE BETTER SCRAM!
VINCENT HERE! I'VE GOT 'EM TREED--86TH AND 3RD; BIERGARTEN HUBIE MENCH.
HARRY VINCENT--KEEP WATCHING THE FRONT EXIT. IT IS UNLIKELY THEY'LL KEEP MISS BAUR THERE LONG, TONIGHT IS OBVIOUSLY THE TRANSPORT NIGHT.
DO NOT ATTEMPT ENTRY. THERE'S A HIGH POWER TRANSMITTER IN THAT BUILDING. A TRANSMITTER I WOULD RATHER THEY DIDN'T DESTROY. I'LL BE THERE SOON.
STAY ON THE LINE FOR BURBANK.

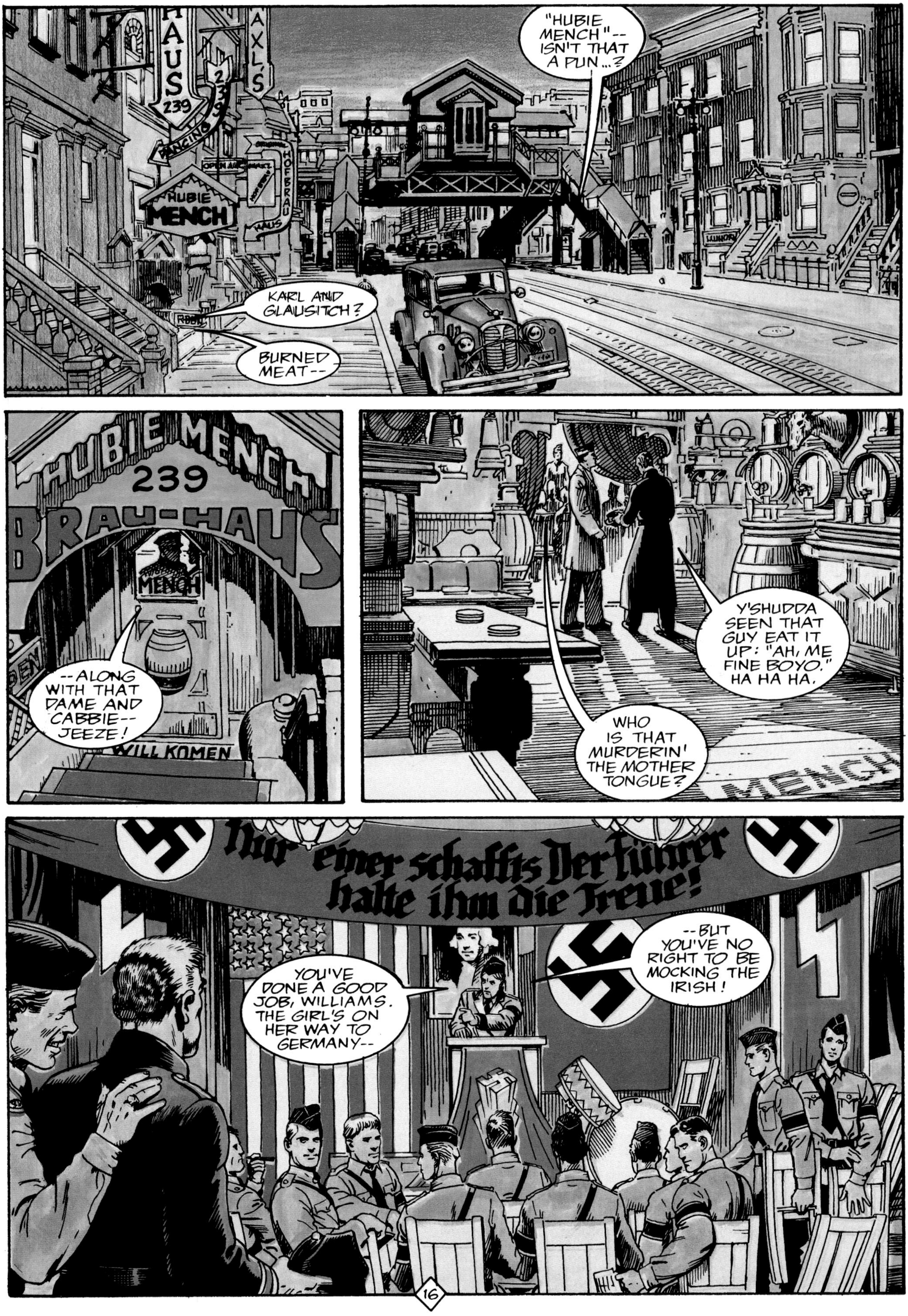
HAUS 239
AXL'S
DANCING
HOFBRAU HAUS
HUBIE MENCH
"HUBIE MENCH"-- ISN'T THAT A PUN...?
KARL AND GLAUSITCH?
BURNED MEAT--
HUBIE MENCH 239 BRAU-HAUS
MENCH
--ALONG WITH THAT DAME AND CABBIE-- JEEZE!
WILL KOMEN
Y'SHUDDA SEEN THAT GUY EAT IT UP: "AH, ME FINE BOYO." HA HA HA.
WHO IS THAT MURDERIN' THE MOTHER TONGUE?
MENCH
Nur einer schaffts Der Fürer
halte ihm die Treue!
YOU'VE DONE A GOOD JOB, WILLIAMS. THE GIRL'S ON HER WAY TO GERMANY--
--BUT YOU'VE NO RIGHT TO BE MOCKING THE IRISH!

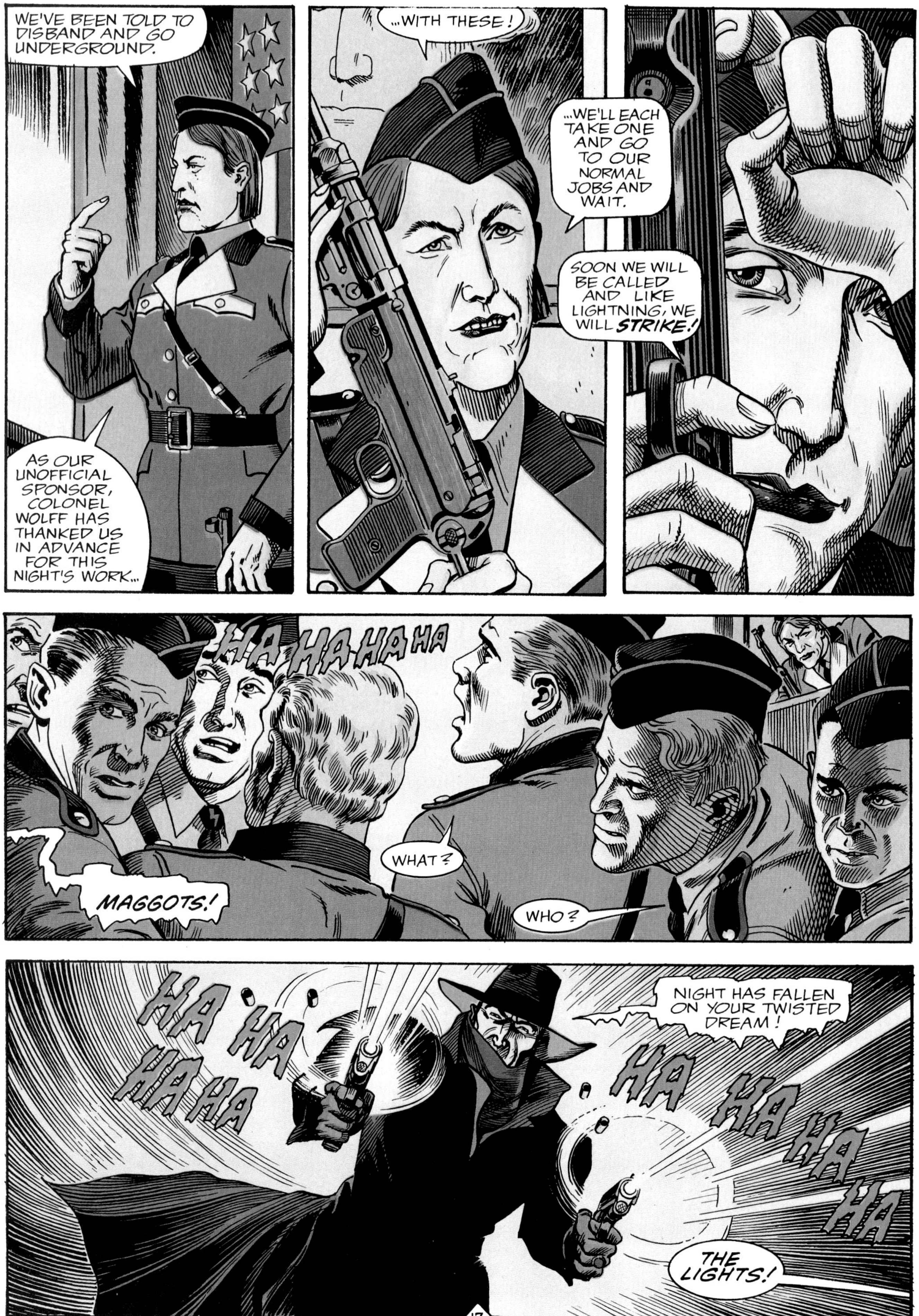

WE'VE BEEN TOLD TO DISBAND AND GO UNDERGROUND.
AS OUR UNOFFICIAL SPONSOR, COLONEL WOLFF HAS THANKED US IN ADVANCE FOR THIS NIGHT'S WORK...
...WITH THESE!
...WE'LL EACH TAKE ONE AND GO TO OUR NORMAL JOBS AND WAIT.
SOON WE WILL BE CALLED AND LIKE LIGHTNING, WE WILL **STRIKE!**
HA HA HA HA HA
MAGGOTS!
WHAT?
WHO?
HA HA HA HA HA HA
NIGHT HAS FALLEN ON YOUR TWISTED DREAM!
HA HA HA HA HA HA HA
THE LIGHTS!

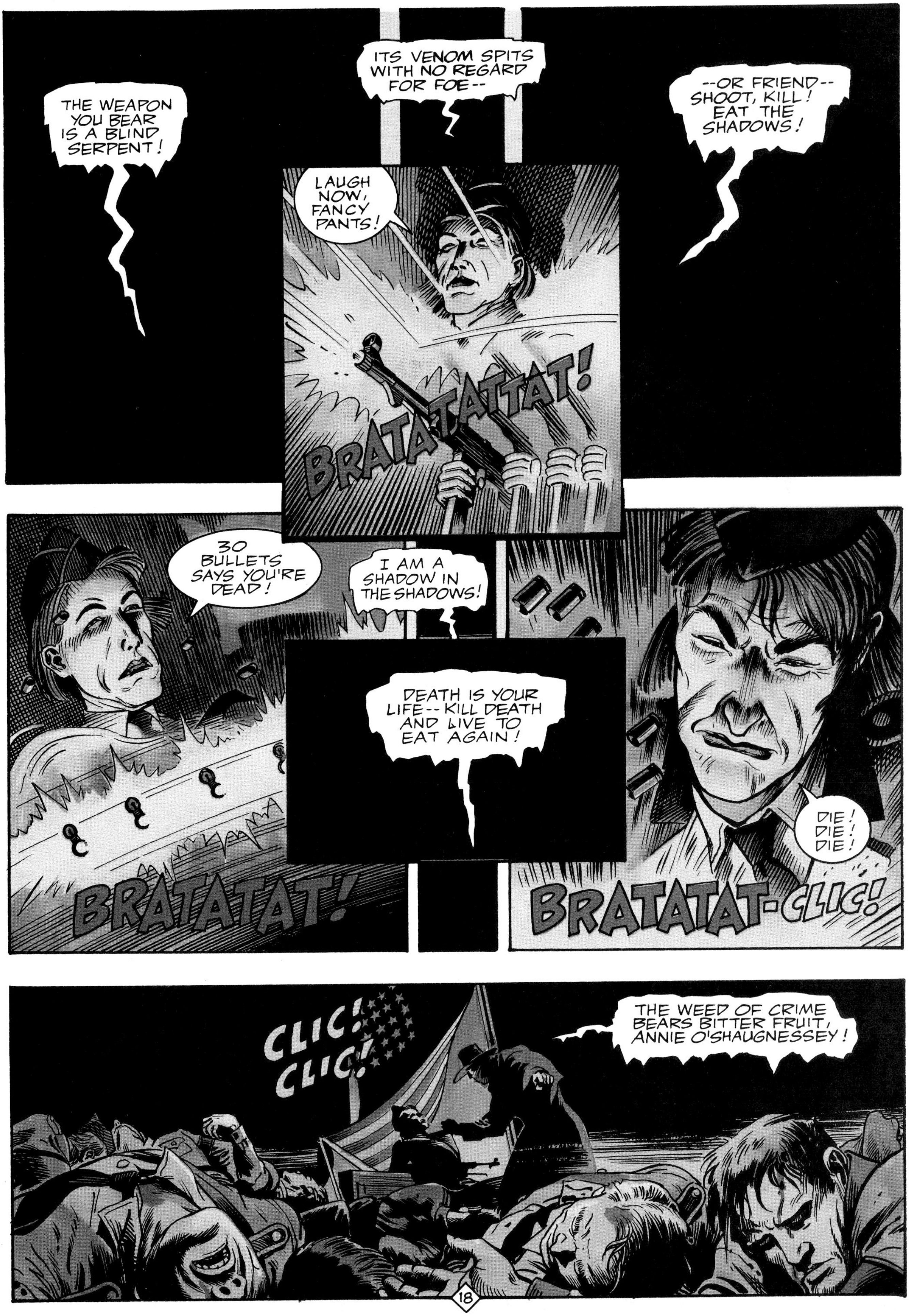
THE WEAPON YOU BEAR IS A BLIND SERPENT!
ITS VENOM SPITS WITH NO REGARD FOR FOE--
--OR FRIEND-- SHOOT, KILL! EAT THE SHADOWS!
LAUGH NOW, FANCY PANTS!
BRATATATTAT!
30 BULLETS SAYS YOU'RE DEAD!
I AM A SHADOW IN THE SHADOWS!
DEATH IS YOUR LIFE--KILL DEATH AND LIVE TO EAT AGAIN!
BRATATAT!
DIE! DIE! DIE!
BRATATAT-CLIC!
CLIC! CLIC!
THE WEED OF CRIME BEARS BITTER FRUIT, ANNIE O'SHAUGNESSEY!

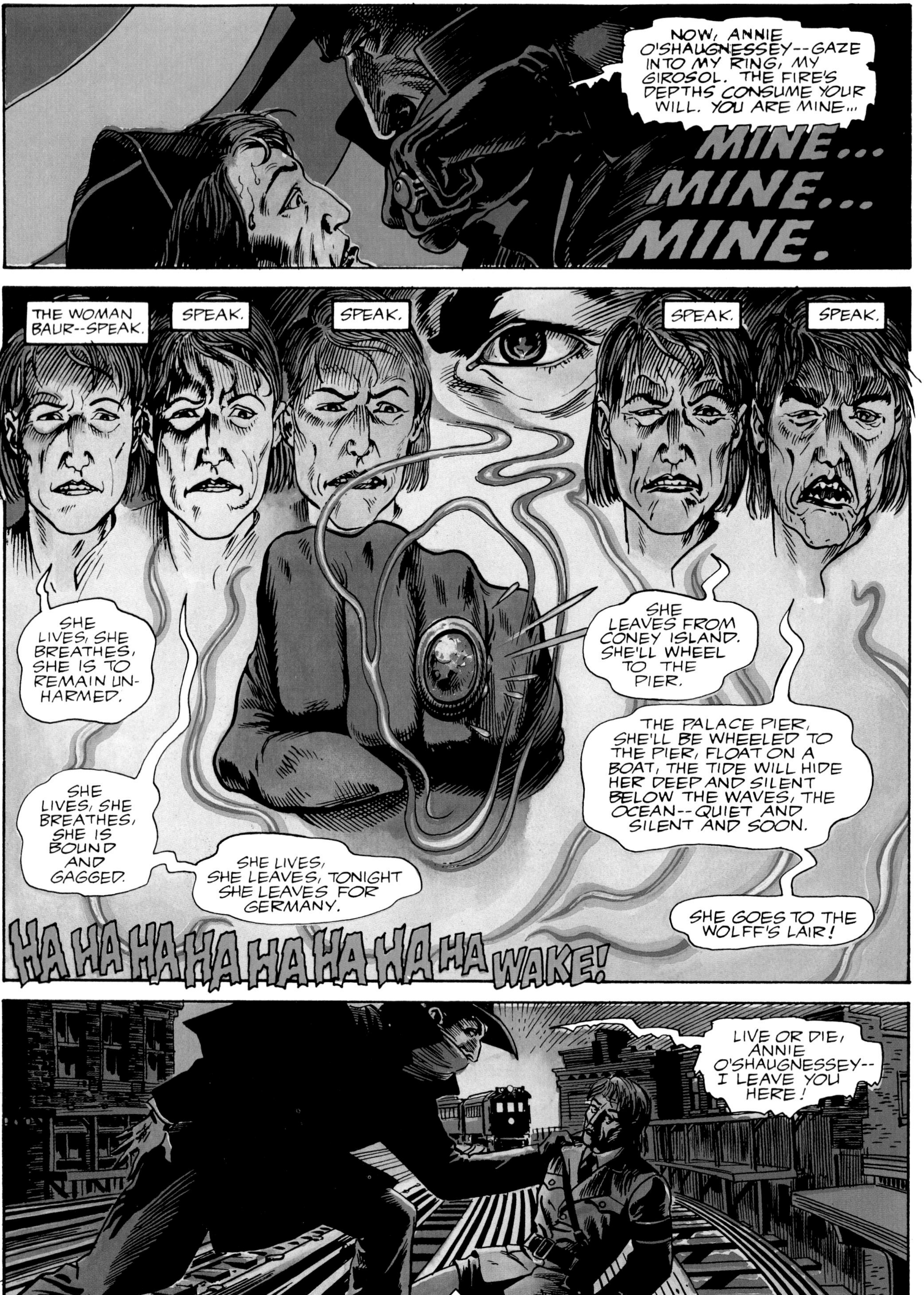
NOW, ANNIE O'SHAUGNESSEY--GAZE INTO MY RING, MY GIROSOL. THE FIRE'S DEPTHS CONSUME YOUR WILL. YOU ARE MINE...
MINE... MINE... MINE.
THE WOMAN BAUR--SPEAK.
SPEAK.
SPEAK.
SPEAK.
SPEAK.
SHE LIVES, SHE BREATHES, SHE IS TO REMAIN UNHARMED.
SHE LIVES, SHE BREATHES, SHE IS BOUND AND GAGGED.
SHE LIVES, SHE LEAVES, TONIGHT SHE LEAVES FOR GERMANY.
SHE LEAVES FROM CONEY ISLAND. SHE'LL WHEEL TO THE PIER.
THE PALACE PIER, SHE'LL BE WHEELED TO THE PIER, FLOAT ON A BOAT, THE TIDE WILL HIDE HER DEEP AND SILENT BELOW THE WAVES, THE OCEAN--QUIET AND SILENT AND SOON.
SHE GOES TO THE WOLFF'S LAIR!
HA HA HA HA HA HA HA HA HA WAKE!
LIVE OR DIE, ANNIE O'SHAUGNESSEY--I LEAVE YOU HERE!

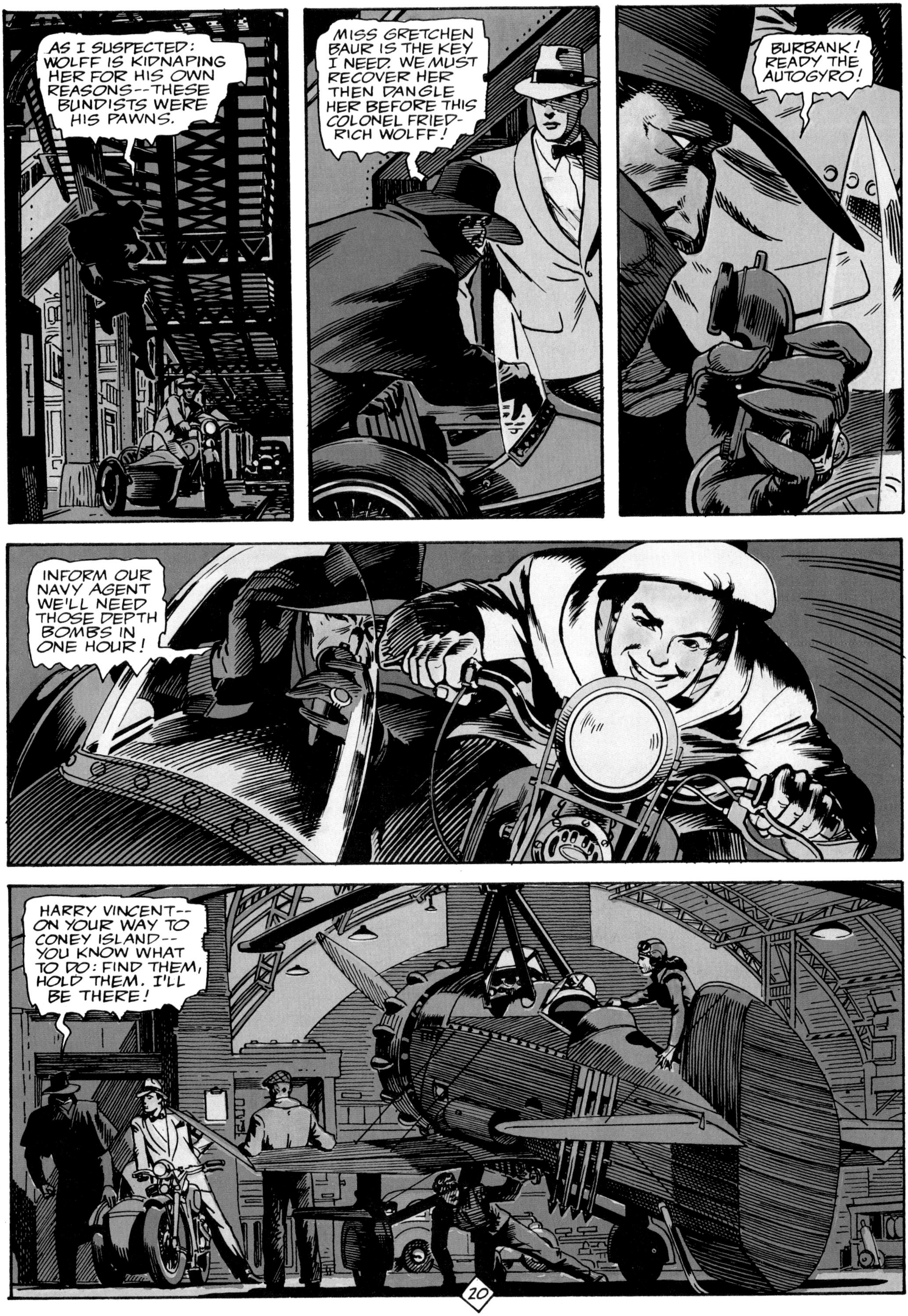
AS I SUSPECTED: WOLFF IS KIDNAPING HER FOR HIS OWN REASONS--THESE BUNDISTS WERE HIS PAWNS.
MISS GRETCHEN BAUR IS THE KEY I NEED. WE MUST RECOVER HER THEN DANGLE HER BEFORE THIS COLONEL FRIED-RICH WOLFF!
BURBANK! READY THE AUTOGYRO!
INFORM OUR NAVY AGENT WE'LL NEED THOSE DEPTH BOMBS IN ONE HOUR!
HARRY VINCENT--ON YOUR WAY TO CONEY ISLAND--YOU KNOW WHAT TO DO: FIND THEM, HOLD THEM. I'LL BE THERE!

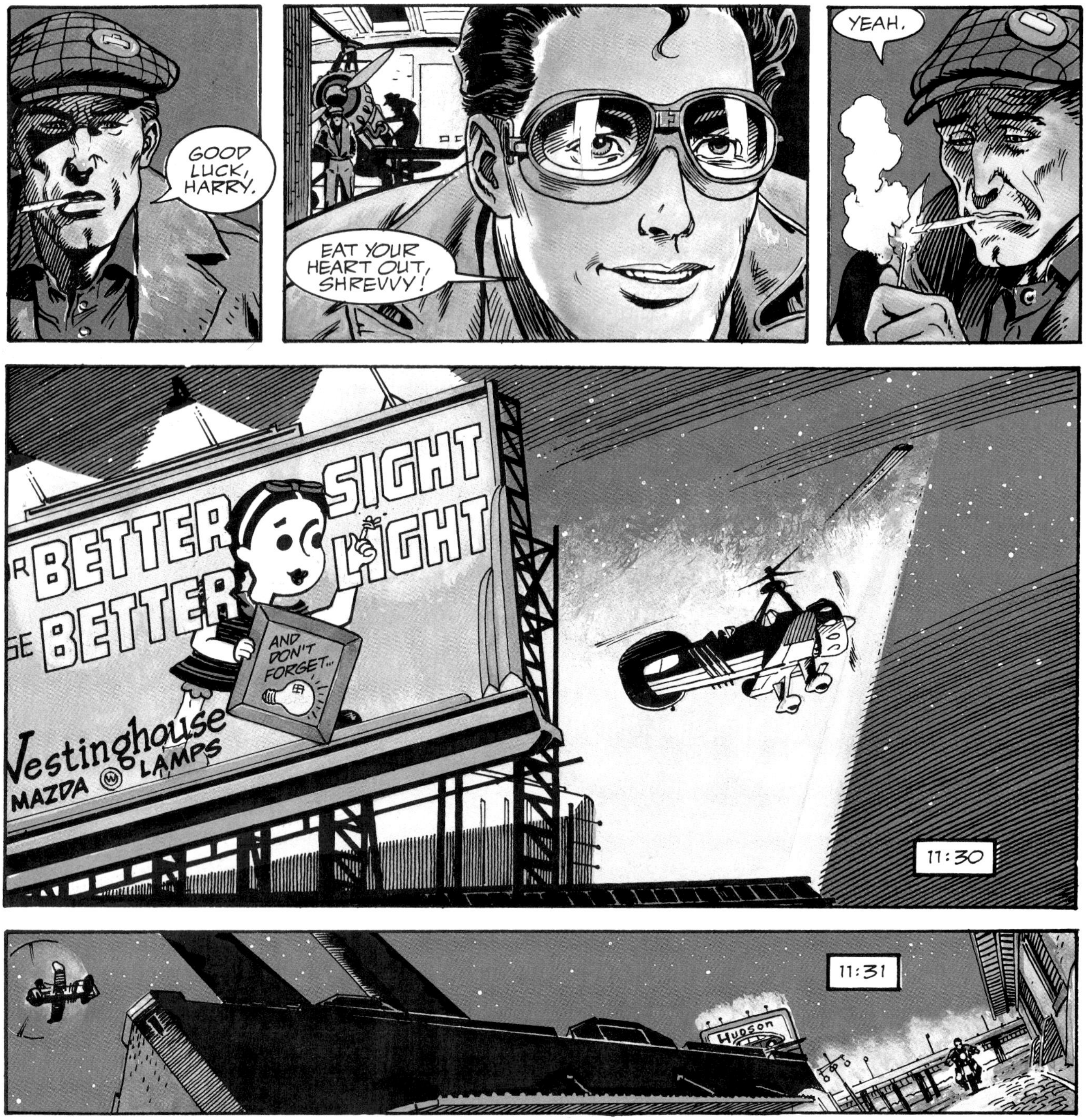
GOOD LUCK, HARRY.
EAT YOUR HEART OUT, SHREVVY!
YEAH.
BETTER SIGHT
BETTER LIGHT
AND DON'T FORGET...
Westinghouse
MAZDA LAMPS
11:30
11:31
Hudson

CONEY ISLAND AMUSEMENT PARK, MIDNIGHT . . .

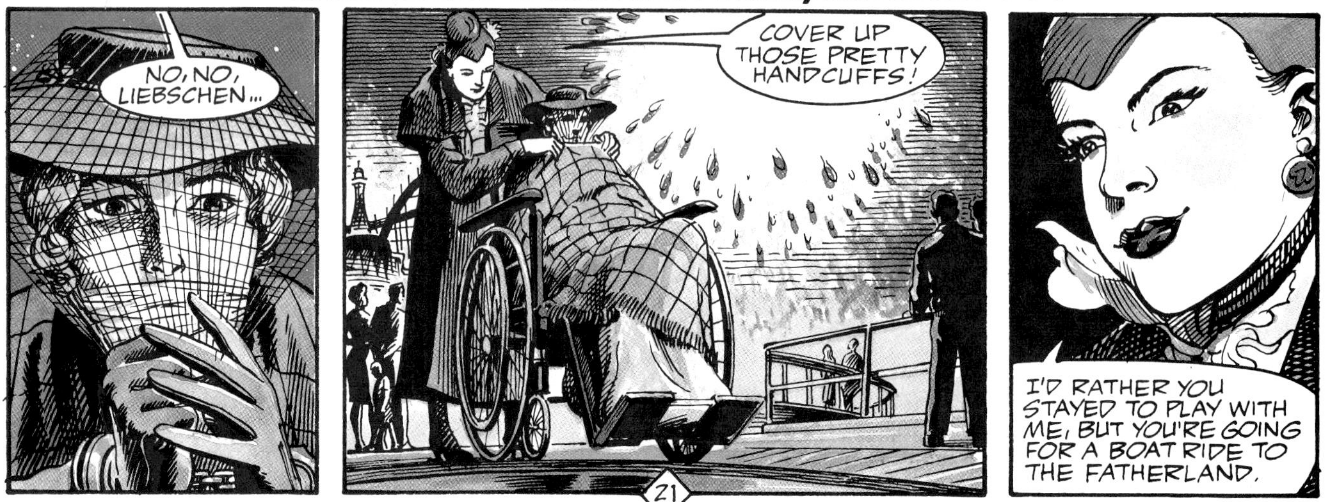
NO, NO, LIEBSCHEN...
COVER UP THOSE PRETTY HANDCUFFS!
I'D RATHER YOU STAYED TO PLAY WITH ME, BUT YOU'RE GOING FOR A BOAT RIDE TO THE FATHERLAND.

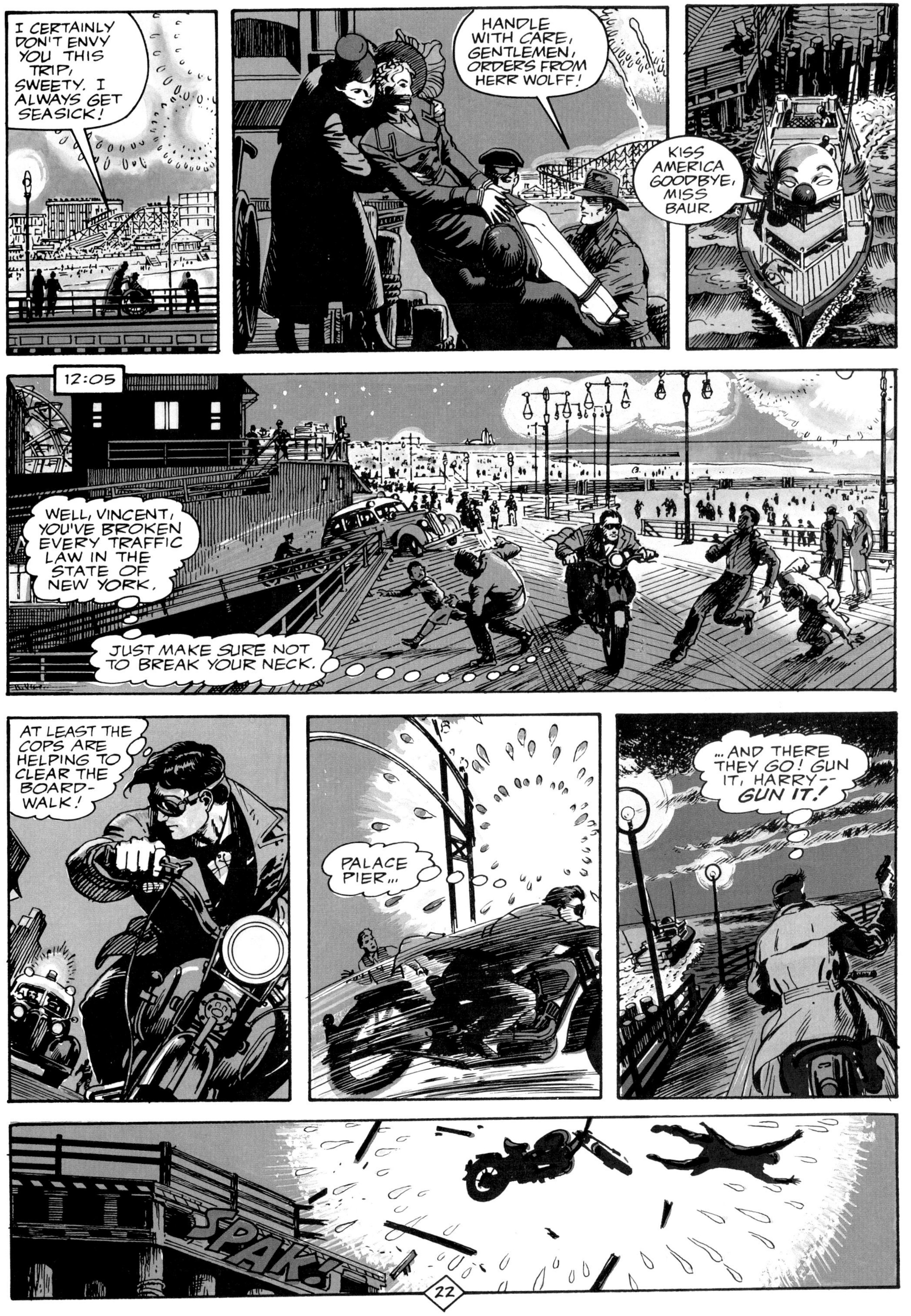
I CERTAINLY DON'T ENVY YOU THIS TRIP, SWEETY. I ALWAYS GET SEASICK!
HANDLE WITH CARE, GENTLEMEN, ORDERS FROM HERR WOLFF!
KISS AMERICA GOODBYE, MISS BAUR.
12:05
WELL, VINCENT, YOU'VE BROKEN EVERY TRAFFIC LAW IN THE STATE OF NEW YORK.
JUST MAKE SURE NOT TO BREAK YOUR NECK.
AT LEAST THE COPS ARE HELPING TO CLEAR THE BOARD-WALK!
PALACE PIER...
...AND THERE THEY GO! GUN IT, HARRY-- GUN IT!
SPAK!

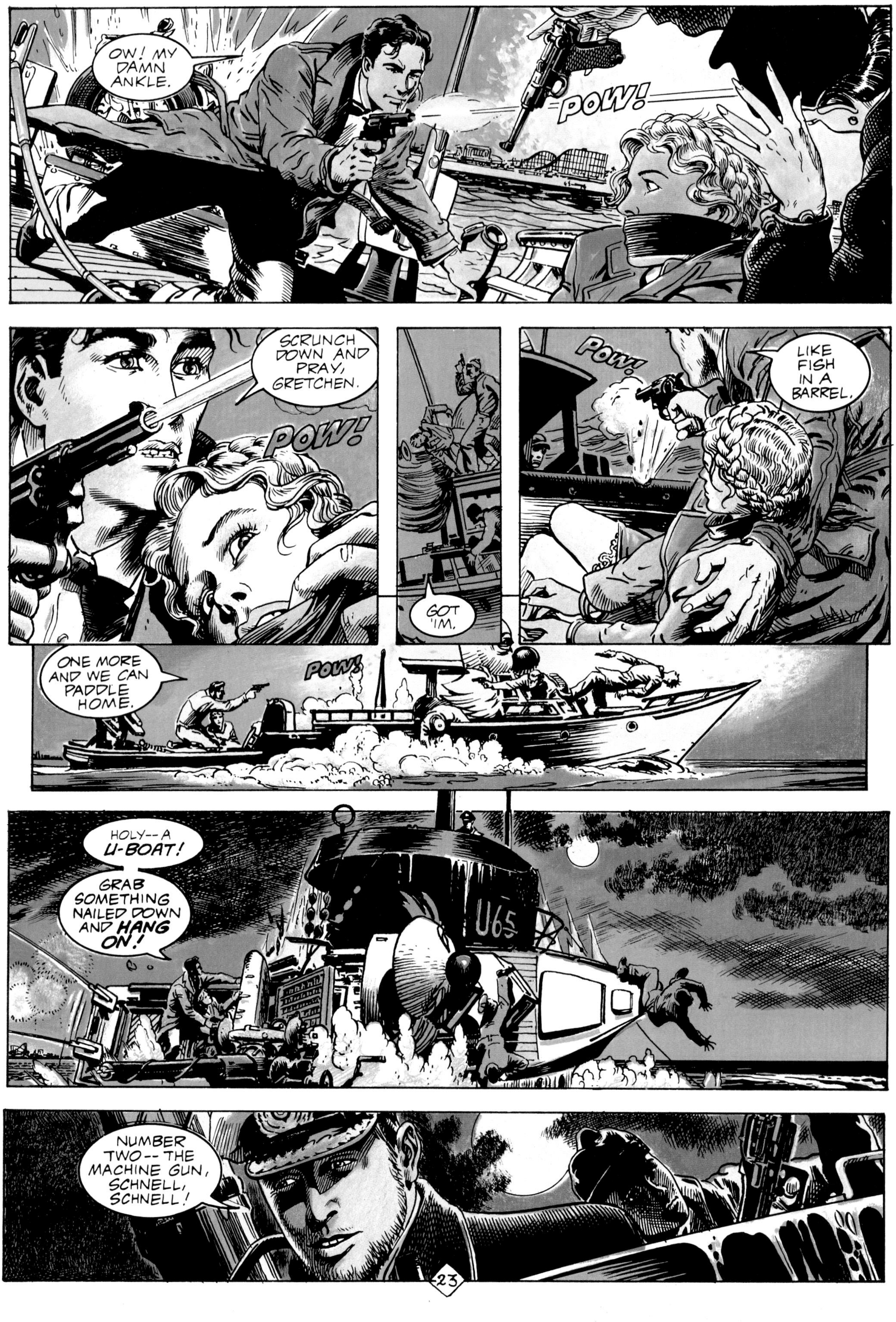
OW! MY DAMN ANKLE.
POW!
SCRUNCH DOWN AND PRAY, GRETCHEN.
POW!
GOT 'IM.
POW!
LIKE FISH IN A BARREL.
ONE MORE AND WE CAN PADDLE HOME.
POW!
HOLY--A U-BOAT!
GRAB SOMETHING NAILED DOWN AND HANG ON!
U65
NUMBER TWO-- THE MACHINE GUN, SCHNELL, SCHNELL!

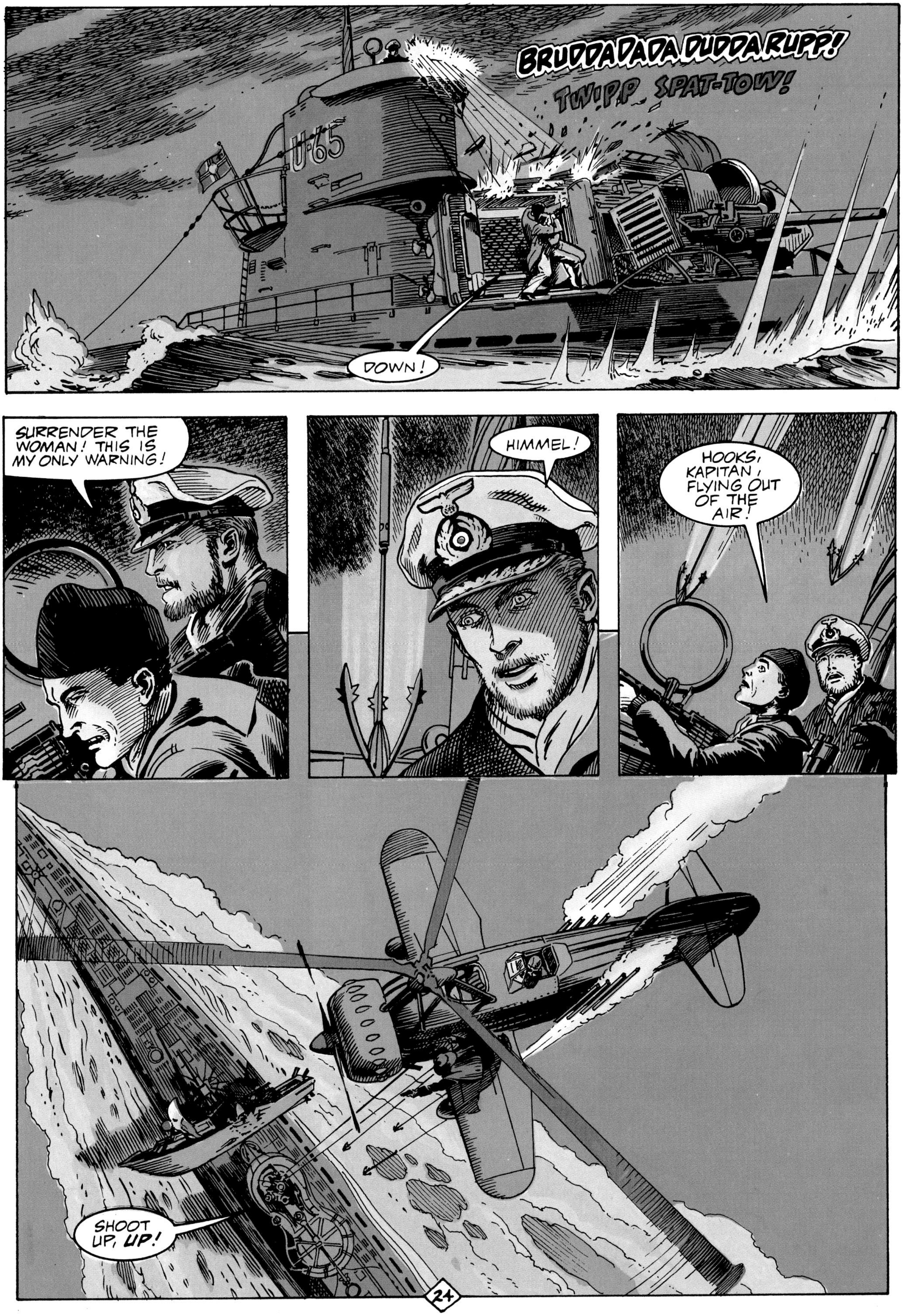
BRUDDADADA DUDDA RUPP!
TWIPP SPAT-TOW!
U-65
DOWN!
SURRENDER THE WOMAN! THIS IS MY ONLY WARNING!
HIMMEL!
HOOKS, KAPITAN, FLYING OUT OF THE AIR!
SHOOT UP, **UP**!

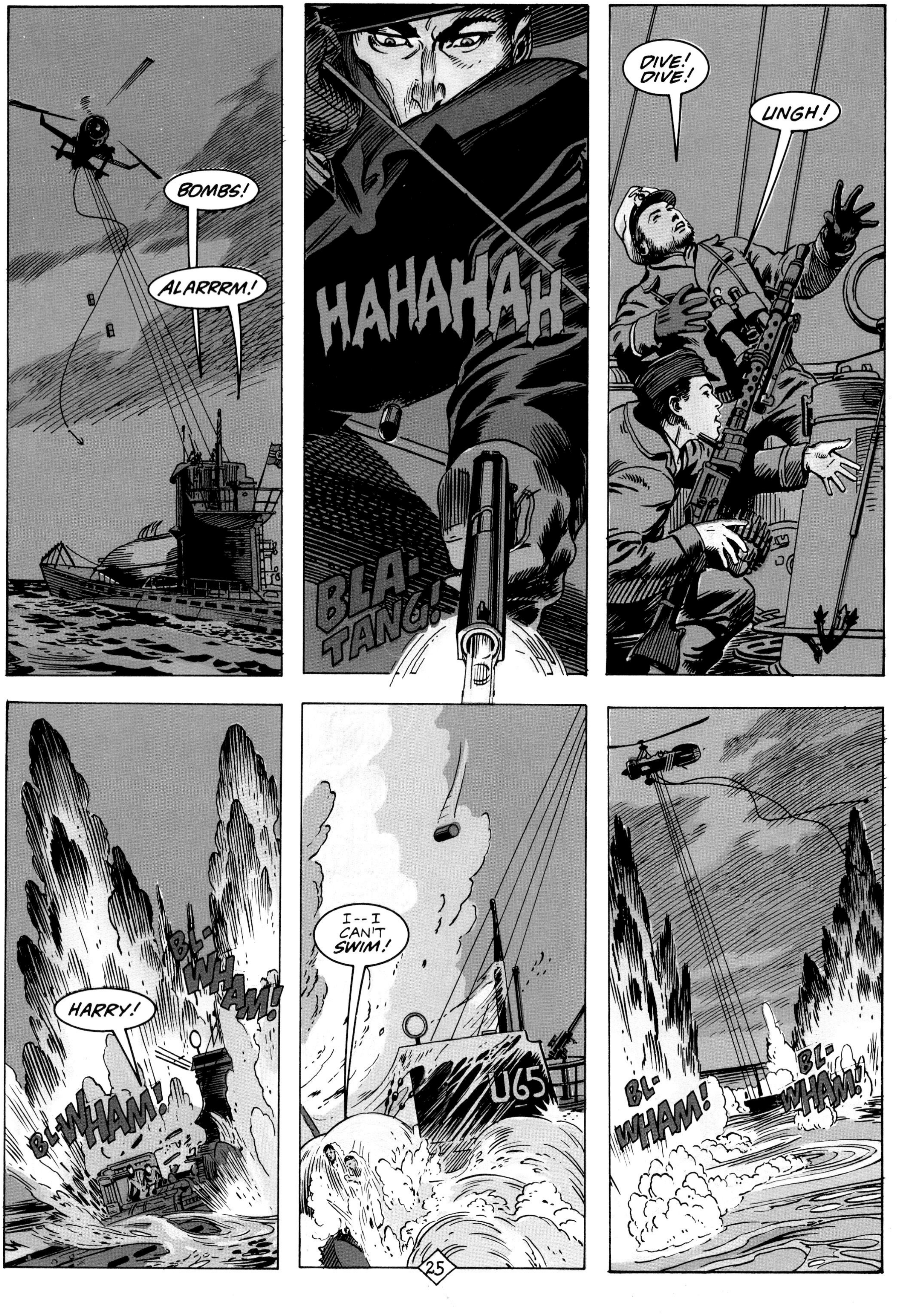
BOMBS!
ALARRRM!
HAHAHAH
BLA-TANG!
DIVE! DIVE!
UNGH!
HARRY!
BL-WHAM!
BL-WHAM!
I--I CAN'T SWIM!
U65
BL-WHAM!
BL-WHAM!

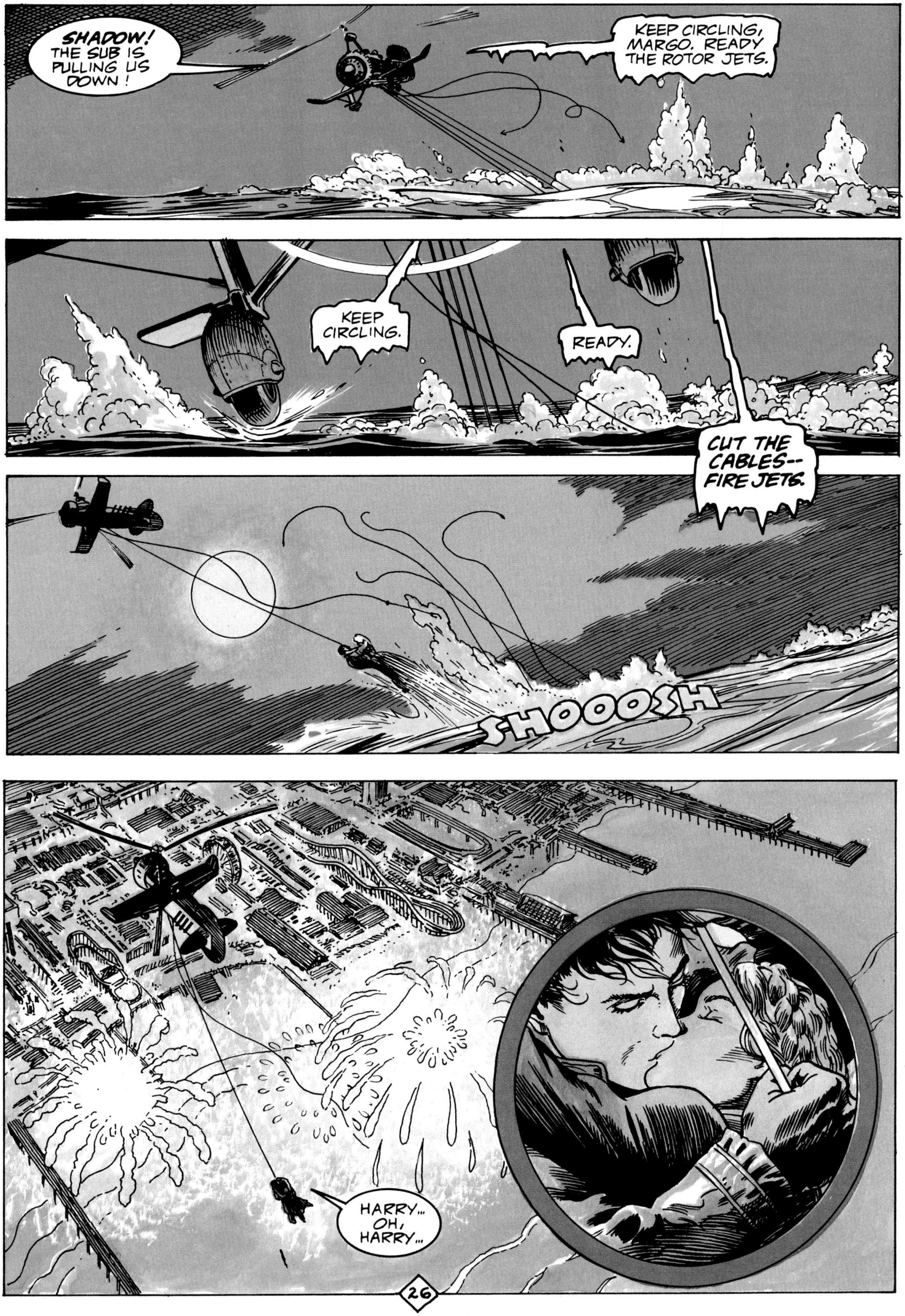
SHADOW! THE SUB IS PULLING US DOWN !
KEEP CIRCLING, MARGO. READY THE ROTOR JETS.
KEEP CIRCLING.
READY.
CUT THE CABLES-- FIRE JETS.
SHOOOSH
HARRY... OH, HARRY...

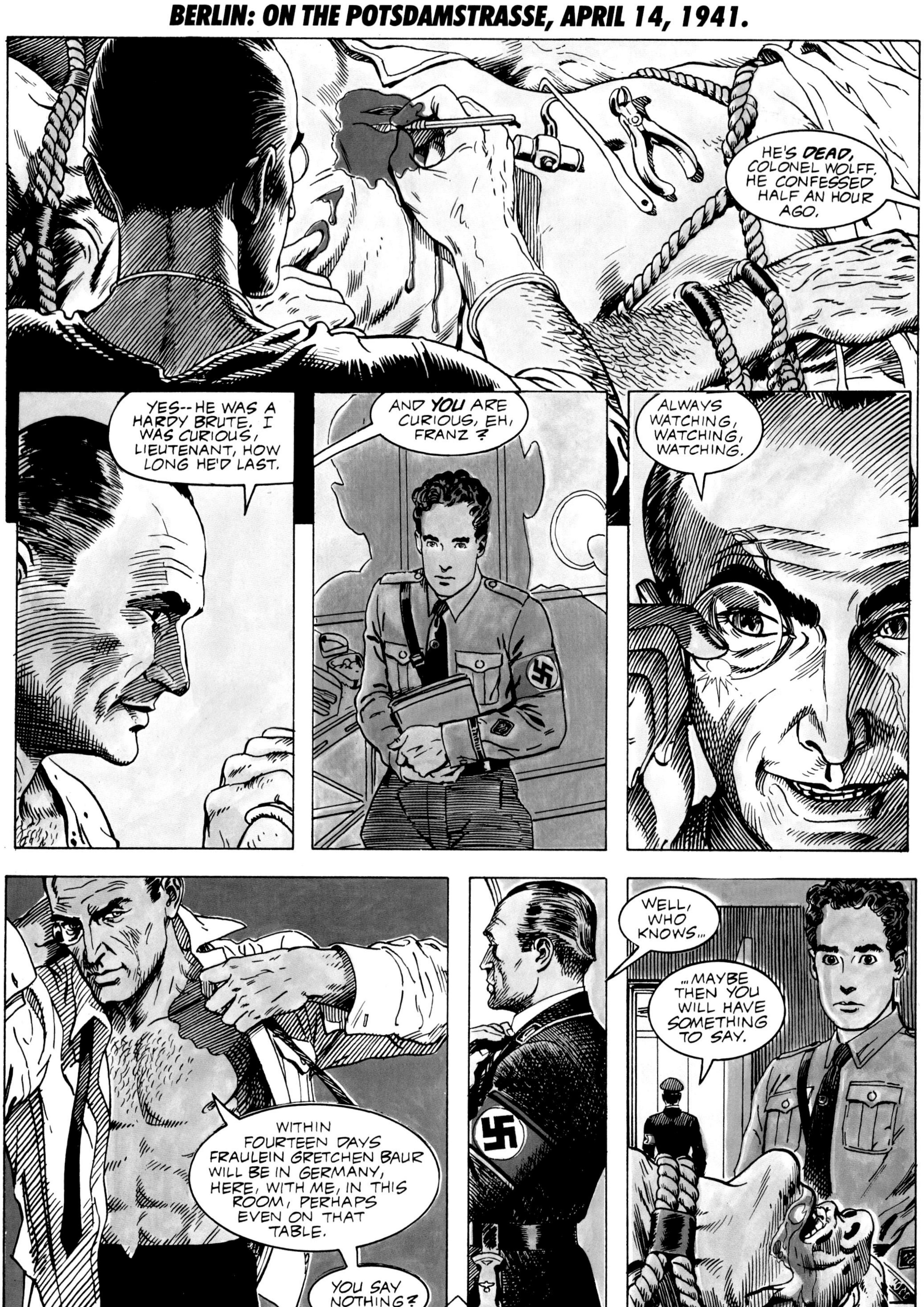
BERLIN: ON THE POTSDAMSTRASSE, APRIL 14, 1941.
HE'S DEAD, COLONEL WOLFF. HE CONFESSED HALF AN HOUR AGO.
YES--HE WAS A HARDY BRUTE. I WAS CURIOUS, LIEUTENANT, HOW LONG HE'D LAST.
AND YOU ARE CURIOUS, EH, FRANZ?
ALWAYS WATCHING, WATCHING, WATCHING.
WITHIN FOURTEEN DAYS FRAULEIN GRETCHEN BAUR WILL BE IN GERMANY, HERE, WITH ME, IN THIS ROOM, PERHAPS EVEN ON THAT TABLE.
YOU SAY NOTHING?
WELL, WHO KNOWS...
...MAYBE THEN YOU WILL HAVE SOMETHING TO SAY.

MANHATTAN: HOTEL ST. REGIS, 5th AVE. & 55th ST.,, APRIL 24, 6 P.M.

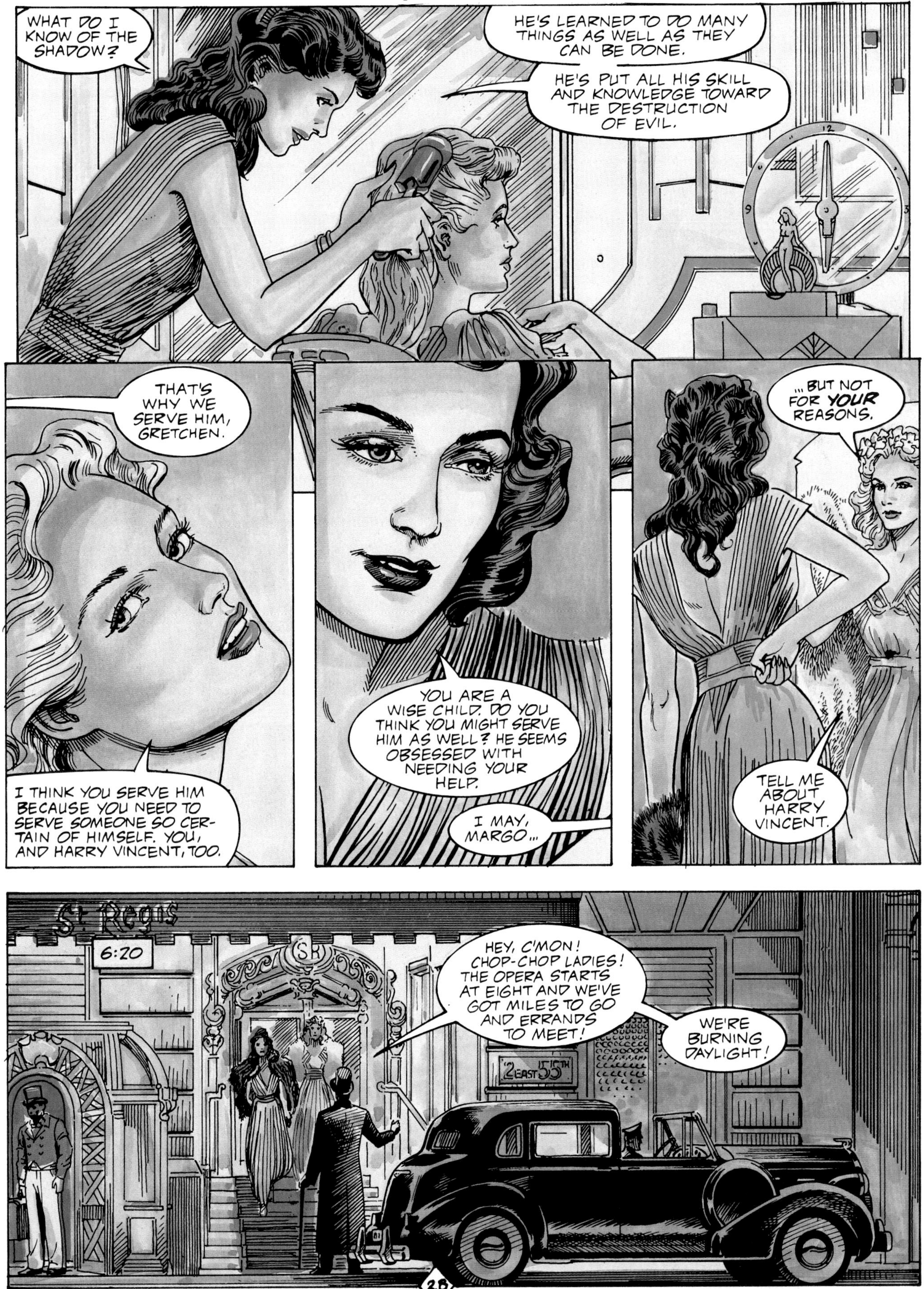

WHAT DO I KNOW OF THE SHADOW?
HE'S LEARNED TO DO MANY THINGS AS WELL AS THEY CAN BE DONE.
HE'S PUT ALL HIS SKILL AND KNOWLEDGE TOWARD THE DESTRUCTION OF EVIL.
THAT'S WHY WE SERVE HIM, GRETCHEN.
I THINK YOU SERVE HIM BECAUSE YOU NEED TO SERVE SOMEONE SO CERTAIN OF HIMSELF. YOU, AND HARRY VINCENT, TOO.
YOU ARE A WISE CHILD. DO YOU THINK YOU MIGHT SERVE HIM AS WELL? HE SEEMS OBSESSED WITH NEEDING YOUR HELP.
I MAY, MARGO...
...BUT NOT FOR YOUR REASONS.
TELL ME ABOUT HARRY VINCENT.
St Regis
6:20
HEY, C'MON! CHOP-CHOP LADIES! THE OPERA STARTS AT EIGHT AND WE'VE GOT MILES TO GO AND ERRANDS TO MEET!
WE'RE BURNING DAYLIGHT!

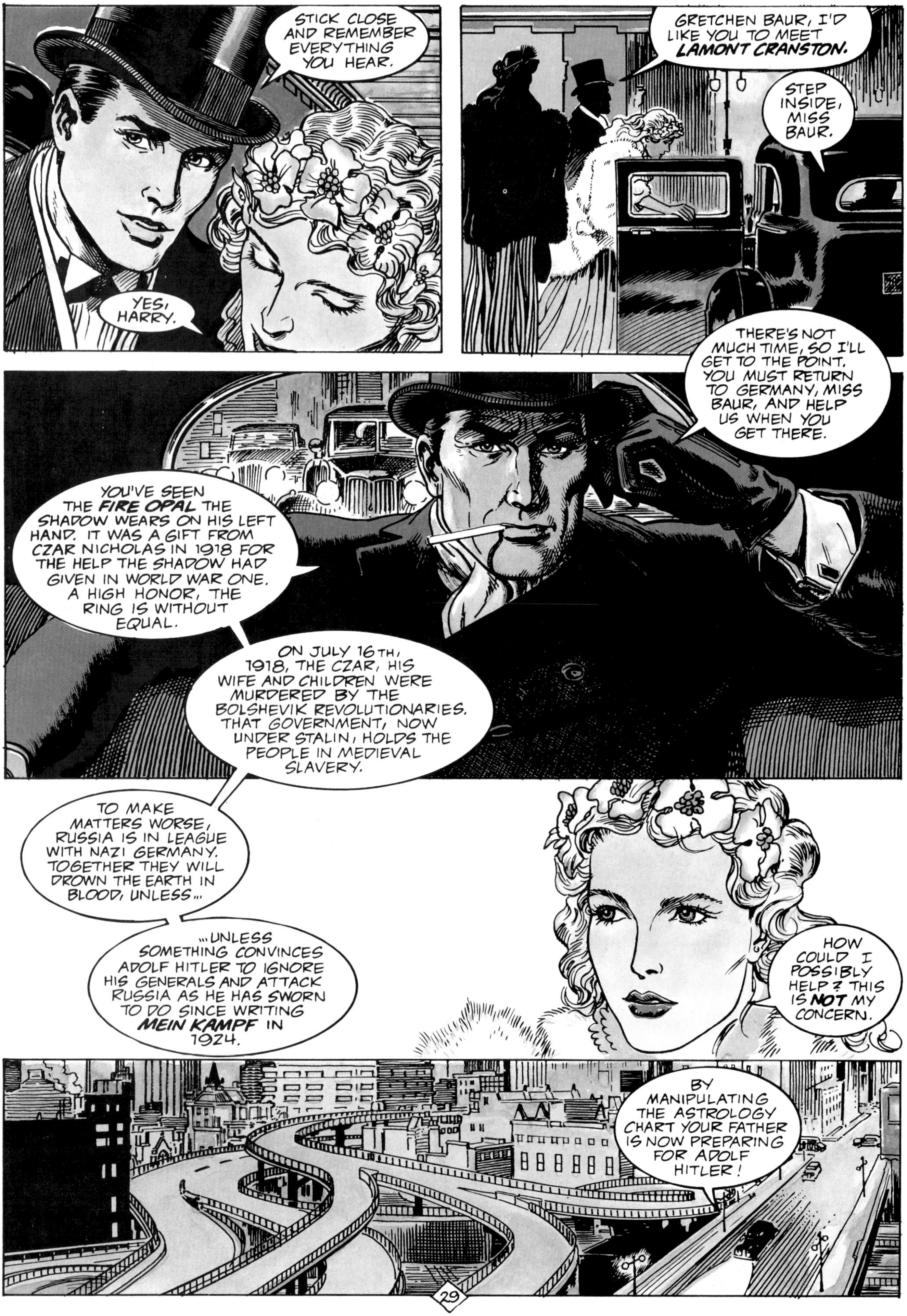
STICK CLOSE AND REMEMBER EVERYTHING YOU HEAR.
YES, HARRY.
GRETCHEN BAUR, I'D LIKE YOU TO MEET LAMONT CRANSTON.
STEP INSIDE, MISS BAUR.
THERE'S NOT MUCH TIME, SO I'LL GET TO THE POINT. YOU MUST RETURN TO GERMANY, MISS BAUR, AND HELP US WHEN YOU GET THERE.
YOU'VE SEEN THE FIRE OPAL THE SHADOW WEARS ON HIS LEFT HAND. IT WAS A GIFT FROM CZAR NICHOLAS IN 1918 FOR THE HELP THE SHADOW HAD GIVEN IN WORLD WAR ONE. A HIGH HONOR, THE RING IS WITHOUT EQUAL.
ON JULY 16TH, 1918, THE CZAR, HIS WIFE AND CHILDREN WERE MURDERED BY THE BOLSHEVIK REVOLUTIONARIES. THAT GOVERNMENT, NOW UNDER STALIN, HOLDS THE PEOPLE IN MEDIEVAL SLAVERY.
TO MAKE MATTERS WORSE, RUSSIA IS IN LEAGUE WITH NAZI GERMANY. TOGETHER THEY WILL DROWN THE EARTH IN BLOOD, UNLESS...
...UNLESS SOMETHING CONVINCES ADOLF HITLER TO IGNORE HIS GENERALS AND ATTACK RUSSIA AS HE HAS SWORN TO DO SINCE WRITING MEIN KAMPF IN 1924.
HOW COULD I POSSIBLY HELP? THIS IS NOT MY CONCERN.
BY MANIPULATING THE ASTROLOGY CHART YOUR FATHER IS NOW PREPARING FOR ADOLF HITLER!

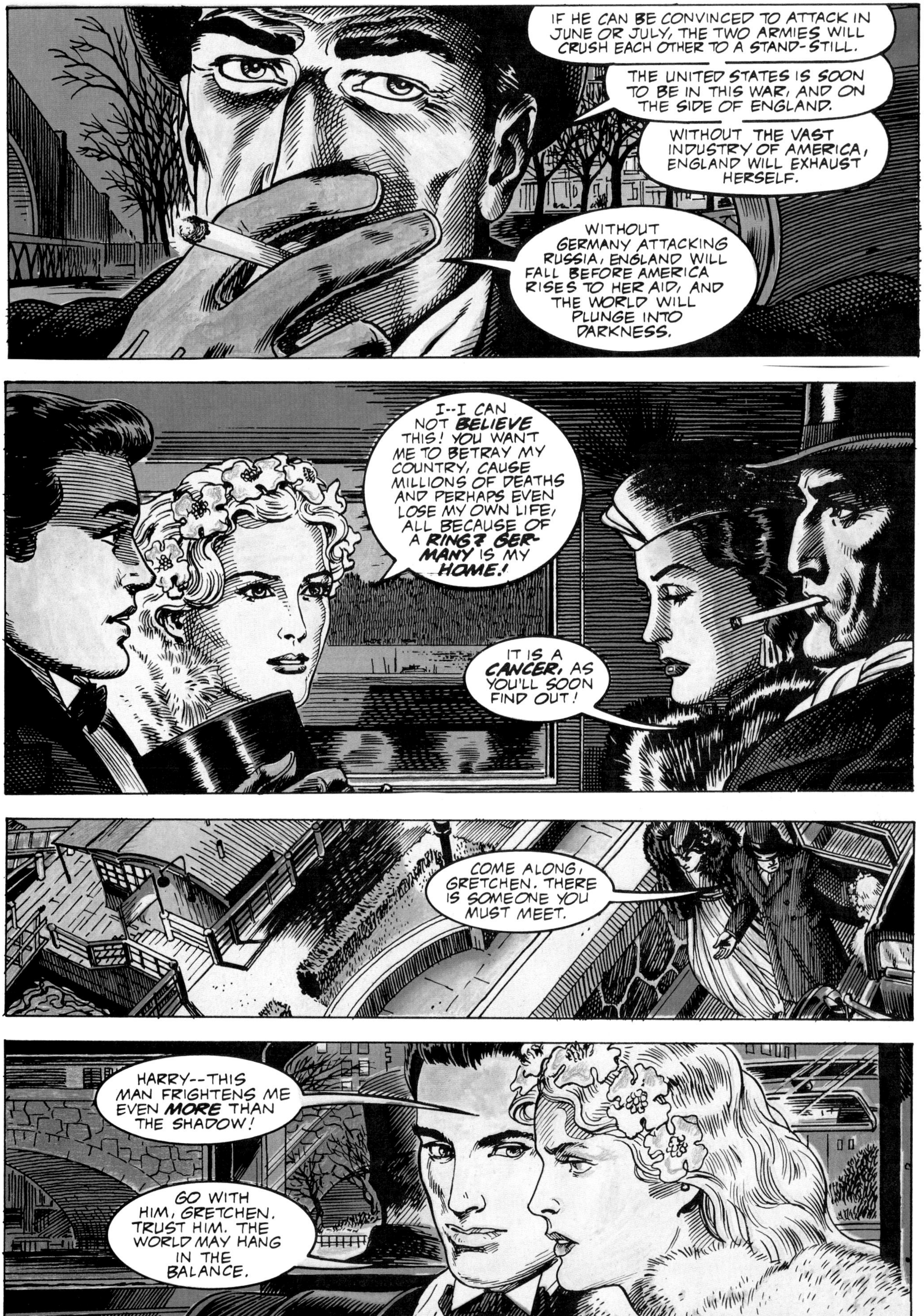

IF HE CAN BE CONVINCED TO ATTACK IN JUNE OR JULY, THE TWO ARMIES WILL CRUSH EACH OTHER TO A STAND-STILL.
THE UNITED STATES IS SOON TO BE IN THIS WAR, AND ON THE SIDE OF ENGLAND.
WITHOUT THE VAST INDUSTRY OF AMERICA, ENGLAND WILL EXHAUST HERSELF.
WITHOUT GERMANY ATTACKING RUSSIA, ENGLAND WILL FALL BEFORE AMERICA RISES TO HER AID, AND THE WORLD WILL PLUNGE INTO DARKNESS.
I--I CAN NOT BELIEVE THIS! YOU WANT ME TO BETRAY MY COUNTRY, CAUSE MILLIONS OF DEATHS AND PERHAPS EVEN LOSE MY OWN LIFE, ALL BECAUSE OF A RING? GERMANY IS MY HOME!
IT IS A CANCER, AS YOU'LL SOON FIND OUT!
COME ALONG, GRETCHEN. THERE IS SOMEONE YOU MUST MEET.
HARRY--THIS MAN FRIGHTENS ME EVEN MORE THAN THE SHADOW!
GO WITH HIM, GRETCHEN. TRUST HIM. THE WORLD MAY HANG IN THE BALANCE.

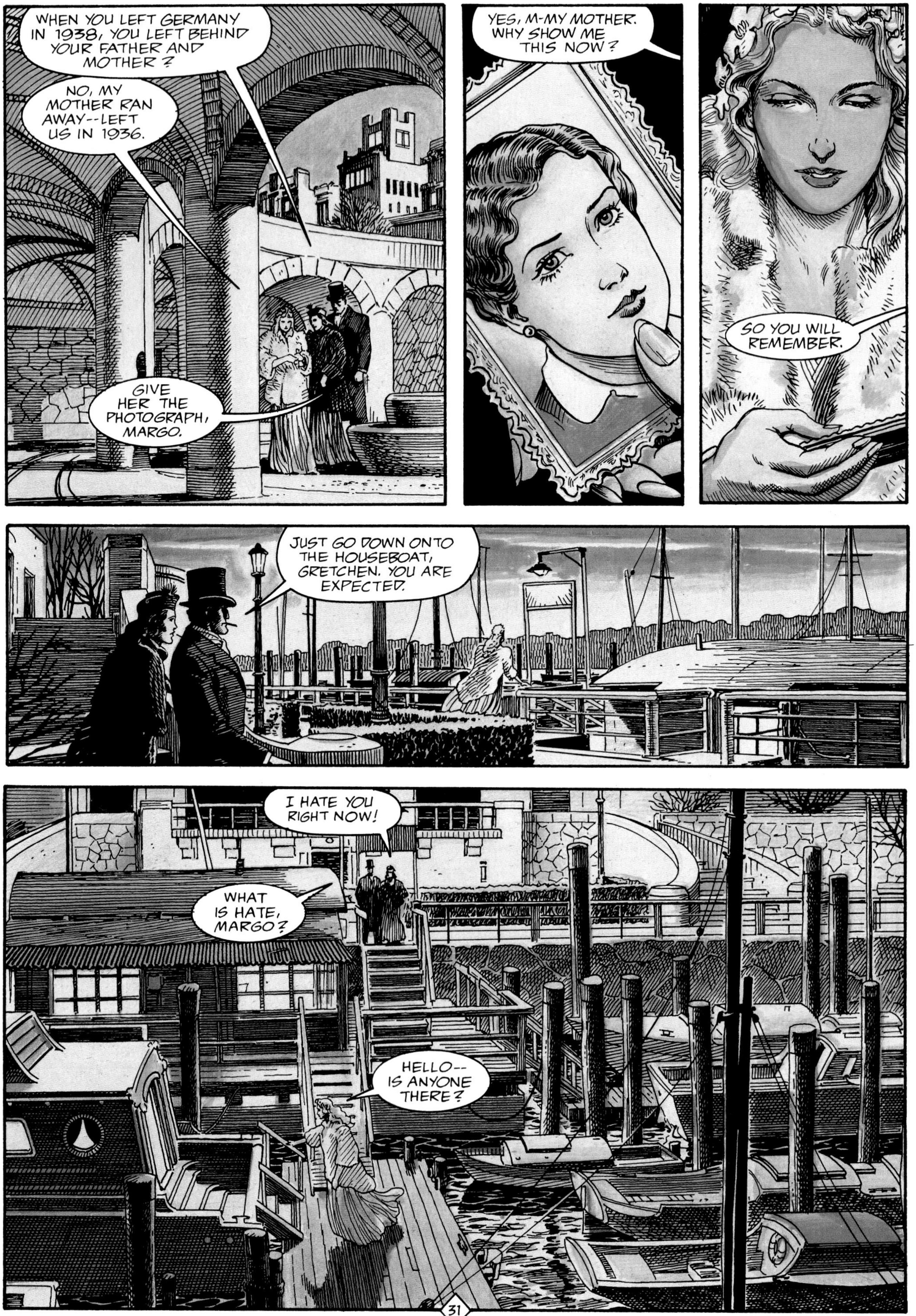
WHEN YOU LEFT GERMANY IN 1938, YOU LEFT BEHIND YOUR FATHER AND MOTHER?
NO, MY MOTHER RAN AWAY--LEFT US IN 1936.
GIVE HER THE PHOTOGRAPH, MARGO.
YES, M-MY MOTHER. WHY SHOW ME THIS NOW?
SO YOU WILL REMEMBER.
JUST GO DOWN ONTO THE HOUSEBOAT, GRETCHEN. YOU ARE EXPECTED.
I HATE YOU RIGHT NOW!
WHAT IS HATE, MARGO?
HELLO-- IS ANYONE THERE?

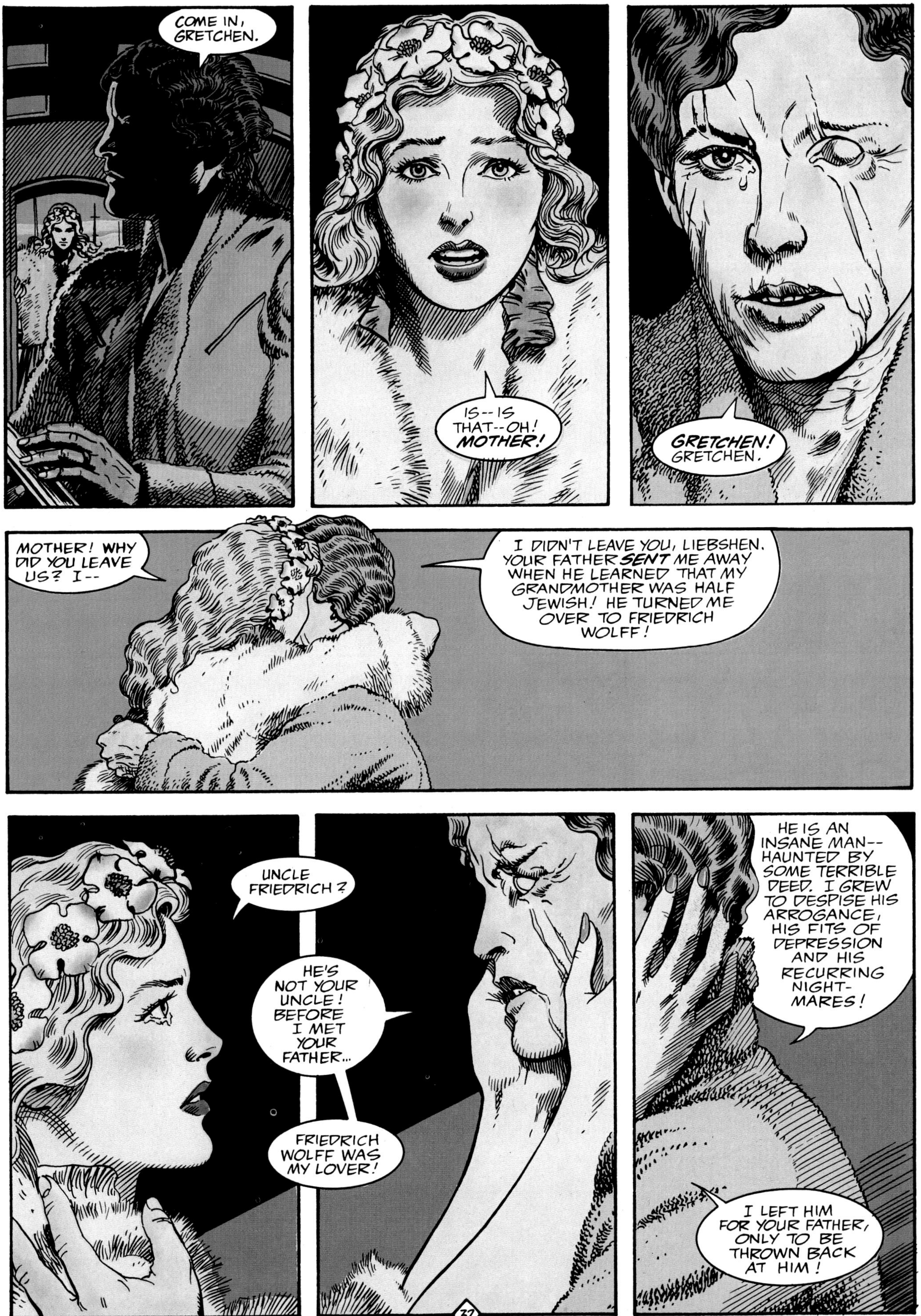

COME IN, GRETCHEN.
IS--IS THAT--OH! MOTHER!
GRETCHEN! GRETCHEN.
MOTHER! WHY DID YOU LEAVE US? I--
I DIDN'T LEAVE YOU, LIEBSHEN. YOUR FATHER SENT ME AWAY WHEN HE LEARNED THAT MY GRANDMOTHER WAS HALF JEWISH! HE TURNED ME OVER TO FRIEDRICH WOLFF!
UNCLE FRIEDRICH?
HE'S NOT YOUR UNCLE! BEFORE I MET YOUR FATHER...
FRIEDRICH WOLFF WAS MY LOVER!
HE IS AN INSANE MAN--HAUNTED BY SOME TERRIBLE DEED. I GREW TO DESPISE HIS ARROGANCE, HIS FITS OF DEPRESSION AND HIS RECURRING NIGHT-MARES!
I LEFT HIM FOR YOUR FATHER, ONLY TO BE THROWN BACK AT HIM!

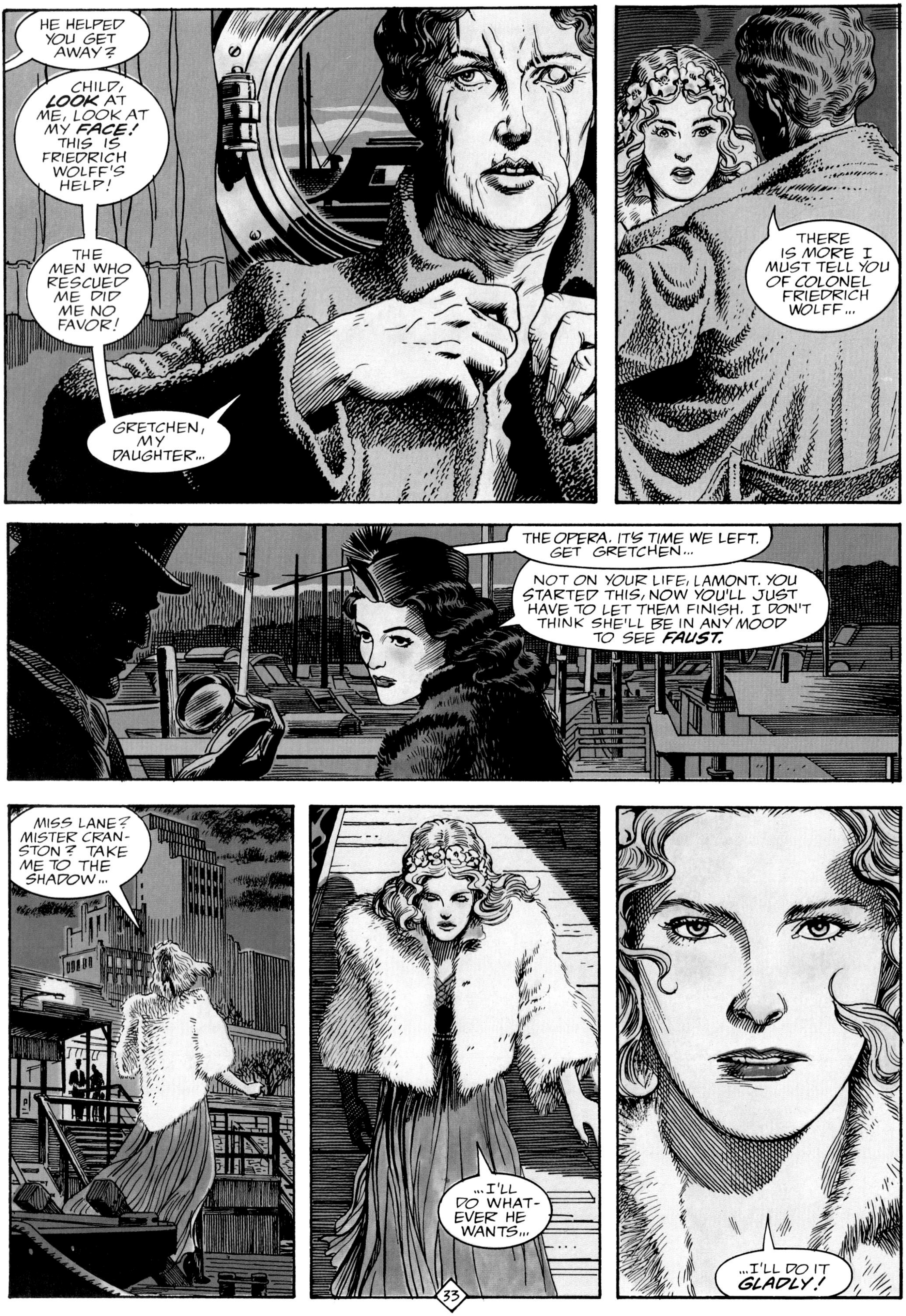
HE HELPED YOU GET AWAY?
CHILD, LOOK AT ME, LOOK AT MY FACE! THIS IS FRIEDRICH WOLFF'S HELP!
THE MEN WHO RESCUED ME DID ME NO FAVOR!
GRETCHEN, MY DAUGHTER...
THERE IS MORE I MUST TELL YOU OF COLONEL FRIEDRICH WOLFF...
THE OPERA. IT'S TIME WE LEFT. GET GRETCHEN...
NOT ON YOUR LIFE, LAMONT. YOU STARTED THIS, NOW YOU'LL JUST HAVE TO LET THEM FINISH. I DON'T THINK SHE'LL BE IN ANY MOOD TO SEE FAUST.
MISS LANE? MISTER CRANSTON? TAKE ME TO THE SHADOW...
...I'LL DO WHATEVER HE WANTS...
...
...I'LL DO IT GLADLY!

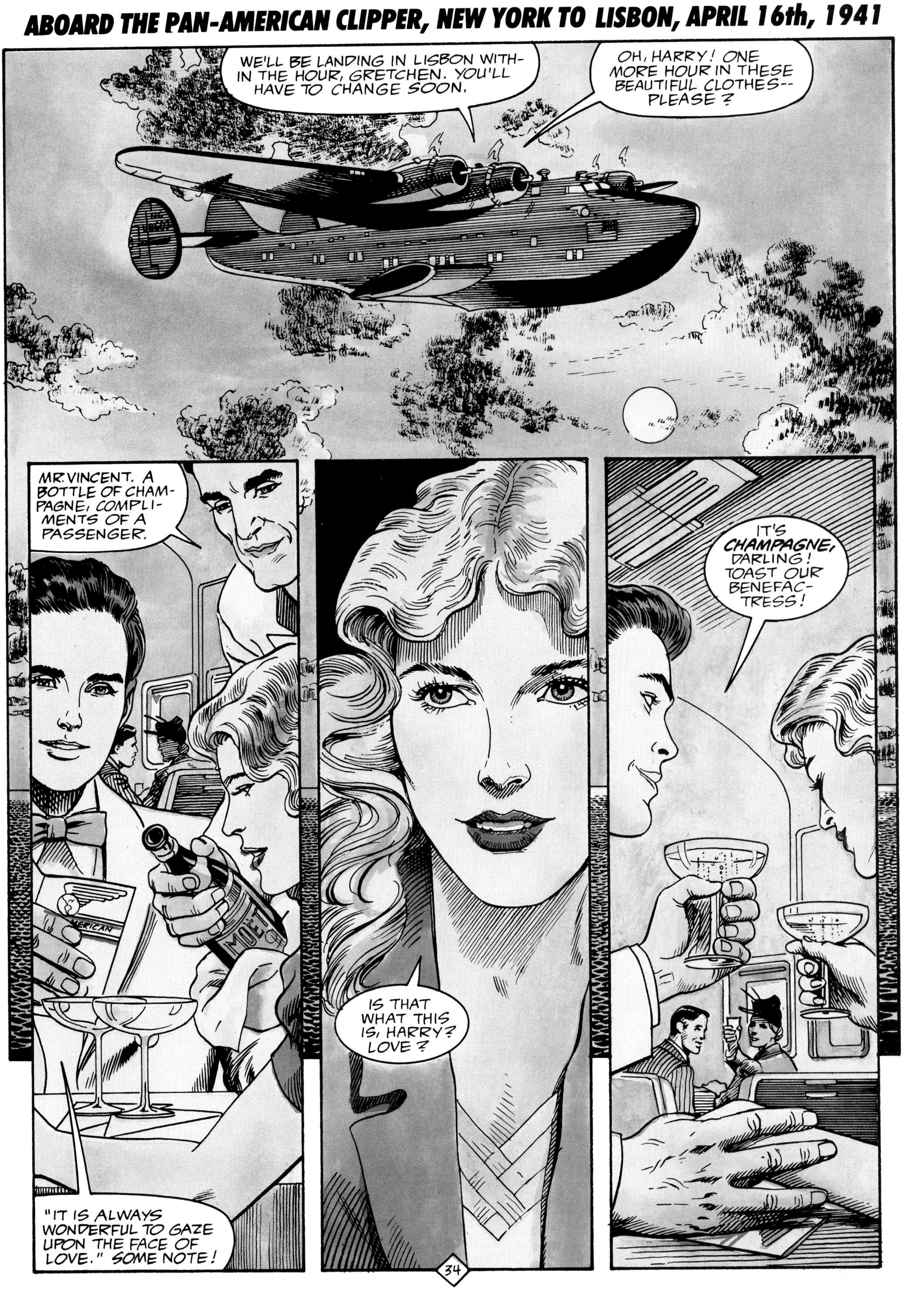
ABOARD THE PAN-AMERICAN CLIPPER, NEW YORK TO LISBON, APRIL 16th, 1941
WE'LL BE LANDING IN LISBON WITHIN THE HOUR, GRETCHEN. YOU'LL HAVE TO CHANGE SOON.
OH, HARRY! ONE MORE HOUR IN THESE BEAUTIFUL CLOTHES--PLEASE?
MR. VINCENT. A BOTTLE OF CHAMPAGNE, COMPLIMENTS OF A PASSENGER.
"IT IS ALWAYS WONDERFUL TO GAZE UPON THE FACE OF LOVE." SOME NOTE!
IS THAT WHAT THIS IS, HARRY? LOVE?
IT'S CHAMPAGNE, DARLING! TOAST OUR BENEFACTRESS!

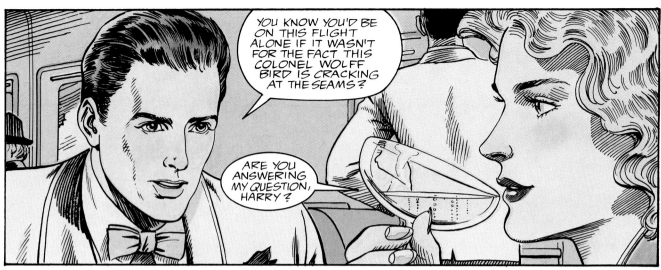

YOU KNOW YOU'D BE ON THIS FLIGHT ALONE IF IT WASN'T FOR THE FACT THIS COLONEL WOLFF BIRD IS CRACKING AT THE SEAMS?

ARE YOU ANSWERING MY QUESTION, HARRY?

PEOPLE ARE WATCHING US. I'VE GOT TO PRETEND THE MONEY I'M TO RECEIVE FOR YOU IS ALL THE PAYMENT I EXPECT, YET I'VE GOT TO STICK CLOSE IN CASE WOLFF DROPS A HINGE.

HE'S PUT HIMSELF INTO A STRANGE POSITION BY GOING BEHIND GOEBBEL'S BACK.

WE'RE GAMBLING THAT IT'S SOMETHING POLITICAL, BUT *HE'S* GAMBLING *TOO*, AND WE WON'T SEE HIS CARDS UNTIL WE GET TO BERLIN!

HARRY. WILL YOU KISS ME?

WE'RE STILL BEING WATCHED...

I DON'T CARE!

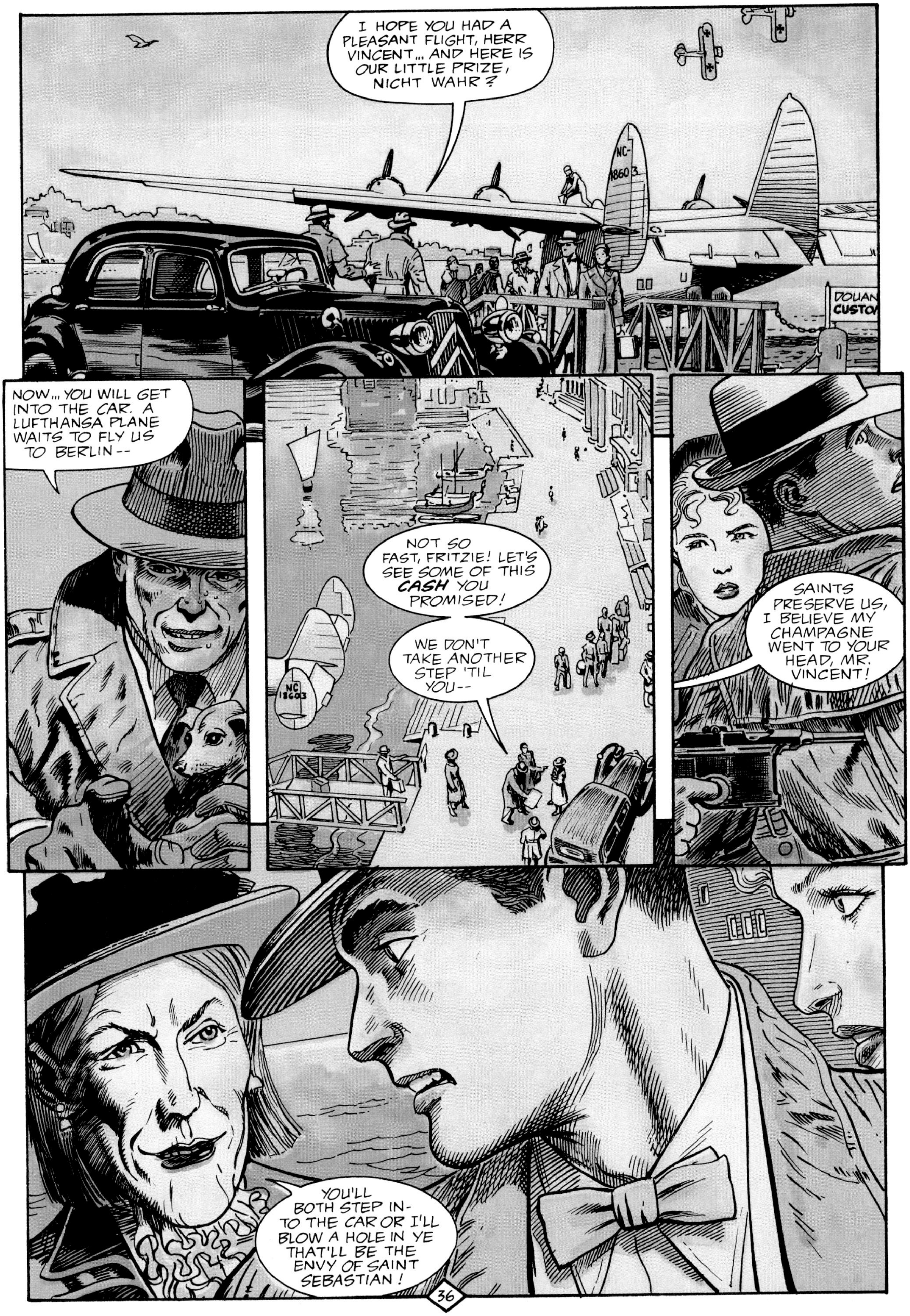
I HOPE YOU HAD A PLEASANT FLIGHT, HERR VINCENT... AND HERE IS OUR LITTLE PRIZE, NICHT WAHR?
NC-18603
DOUAN
CUSTO
NOW... YOU WILL GET INTO THE CAR. A LUFTHANSA PLANE WAITS TO FLY US TO BERLIN--
NOT SO FAST, FRITZIE! LET'S SEE SOME OF THIS **CASH** YOU PROMISED!
WE DON'T TAKE ANOTHER STEP 'TIL YOU--
NC 18603
SAINTS PRESERVE US, I BELIEVE MY CHAMPAGNE WENT TO YOUR HEAD, MR. VINCENT!
YOU'LL BOTH STEP IN-TO THE CAR OR I'LL BLOW A HOLE IN YE THAT'LL BE THE ENVY OF SAINT SEBASTIAN!

BERLIN: RADIO ROOM OF THE AUSLANDER ORGANIZATION, 10 PM

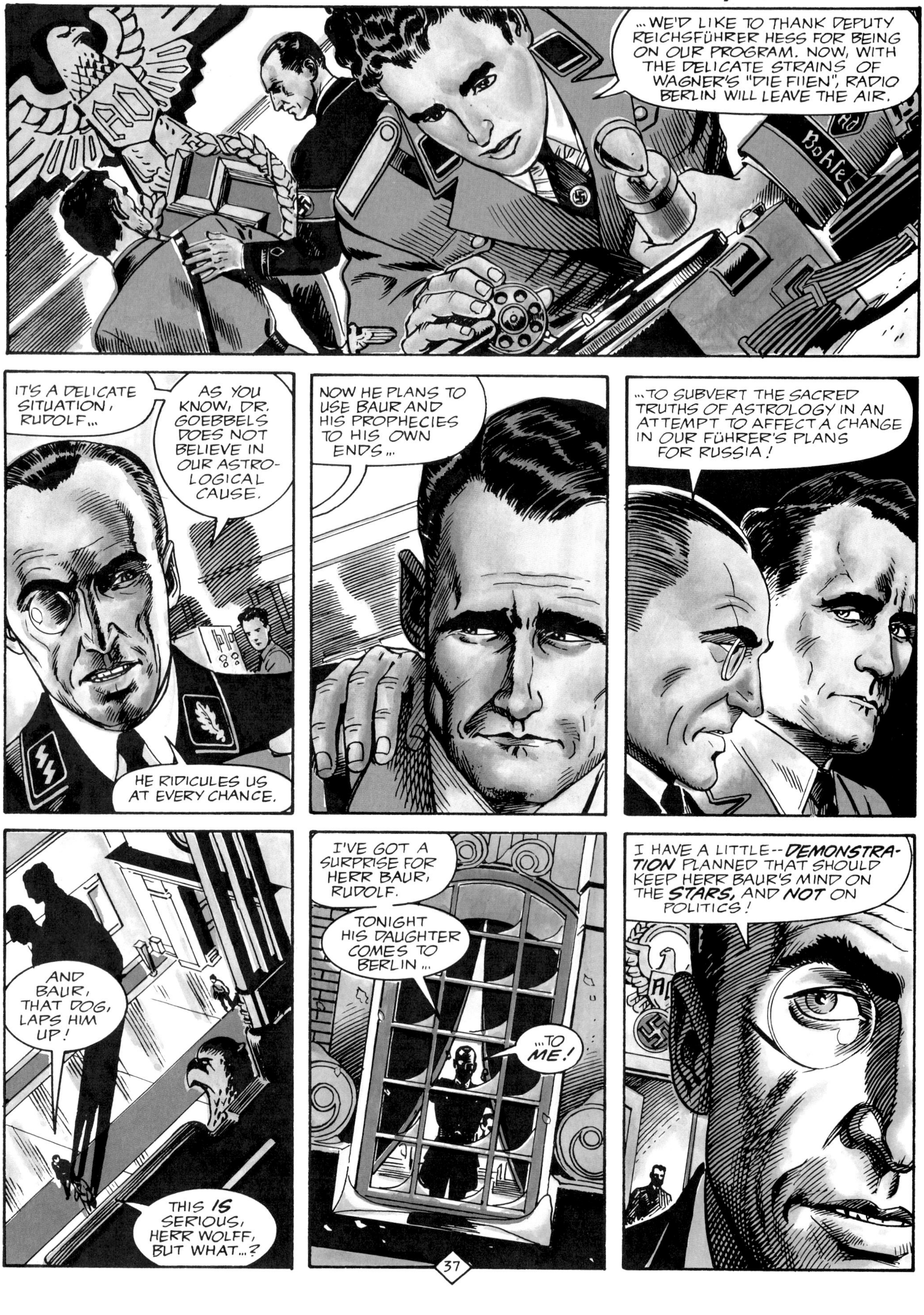
...WE'D LIKE TO THANK DEPUTY REICHSFÜHRER HESS FOR BEING ON OUR PROGRAM. NOW, WITH THE DELICATE STRAINS OF WAGNER'S "DIE FIIEN", RADIO BERLIN WILL LEAVE THE AIR.
IT'S A DELICATE SITUATION, RUDOLF...
AS YOU KNOW, DR. GOEBBELS DOES NOT BELIEVE IN OUR ASTROLOGICAL CAUSE.
HE RIDICULES US AT EVERY CHANCE.
NOW HE PLANS TO USE BAUR AND HIS PROPHECIES TO HIS OWN ENDS...
...TO SUBVERT THE SACRED TRUTHS OF ASTROLOGY IN AN ATTEMPT TO AFFECT A CHANGE IN OUR FÜHRER'S PLANS FOR RUSSIA!
AND BAUR, THAT DOG, LAPS HIM UP!
THIS IS SERIOUS, HERR WOLFF, BUT WHAT...?
I'VE GOT A SURPRISE FOR HERR BAUR, RUDOLF.
TONIGHT HIS DAUGHTER COMES TO BERLIN...
...TO ME!
I HAVE A LITTLE--DEMONSTRATION PLANNED THAT SHOULD KEEP HERR BAUR'S MIND ON THE STARS, AND NOT ON POLITICS!

YOU MUST BE THERE, RUDOLF. YOU ARE THE GREAT ARBITER!

YOU ARE THE FÜHRER'S OLDEST FRIEND!

YOU LED THE CHARGE AT MUNICH!

YOU WROTE IN PRISON AS HE DICTATED MEIN KAMPF!

WHY SHOULD UPSTARTS LIKE GOEBBELS TURN THE FÜHRER'S EAR FROM YOU?

PUT ME THROUGH TO DR. GOEBBELS!

DOKTOR, I...

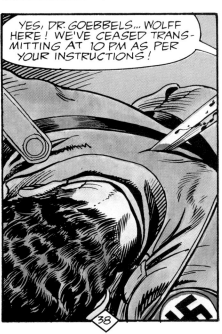

YES, DR. GOEBBELS... WOLFF HERE! WE'VE CEASED TRANSMITTING AT 10 PM AS PER YOUR INSTRUCTIONS!

YES... AND GOOD NIGHT TO YOU, DOKTOR.

38

BERLIN: TEMPLEHOF AIRPORT, 11 PM, APRIL 1941 . . .

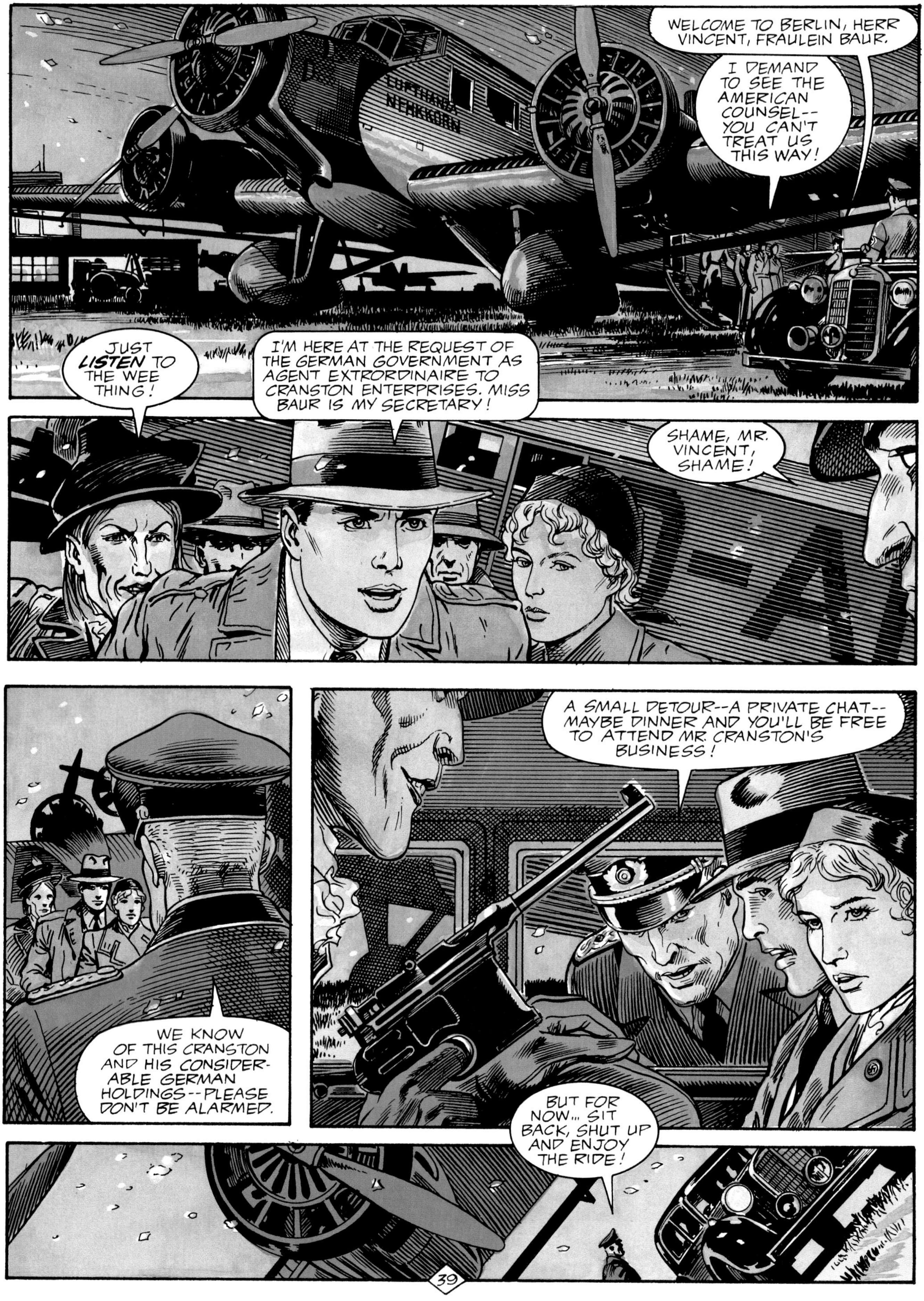

WELCOME TO BERLIN, HERR VINCENT, FRAULEIN BAUR.
I DEMAND TO SEE THE AMERICAN COUNSEL-- YOU CAN'T TREAT US THIS WAY!
JUST LISTEN TO THE WEE THING!
I'M HERE AT THE REQUEST OF THE GERMAN GOVERNMENT AS AGENT EXTRORDINAIRE TO CRANSTON ENTERPRISES. MISS BAUR IS MY SECRETARY!
SHAME, MR. VINCENT, SHAME!
WE KNOW OF THIS CRANSTON AND HIS CONSIDER-ABLE GERMAN HOLDINGS--PLEASE DON'T BE ALARMED.
A SMALL DETOUR--A PRIVATE CHAT--MAYBE DINNER AND YOU'LL BE FREE TO ATTEND MR. CRANSTON'S BUSINESS!
BUT FOR NOW... SIT BACK, SHUT UP AND ENJOY THE RIDE!

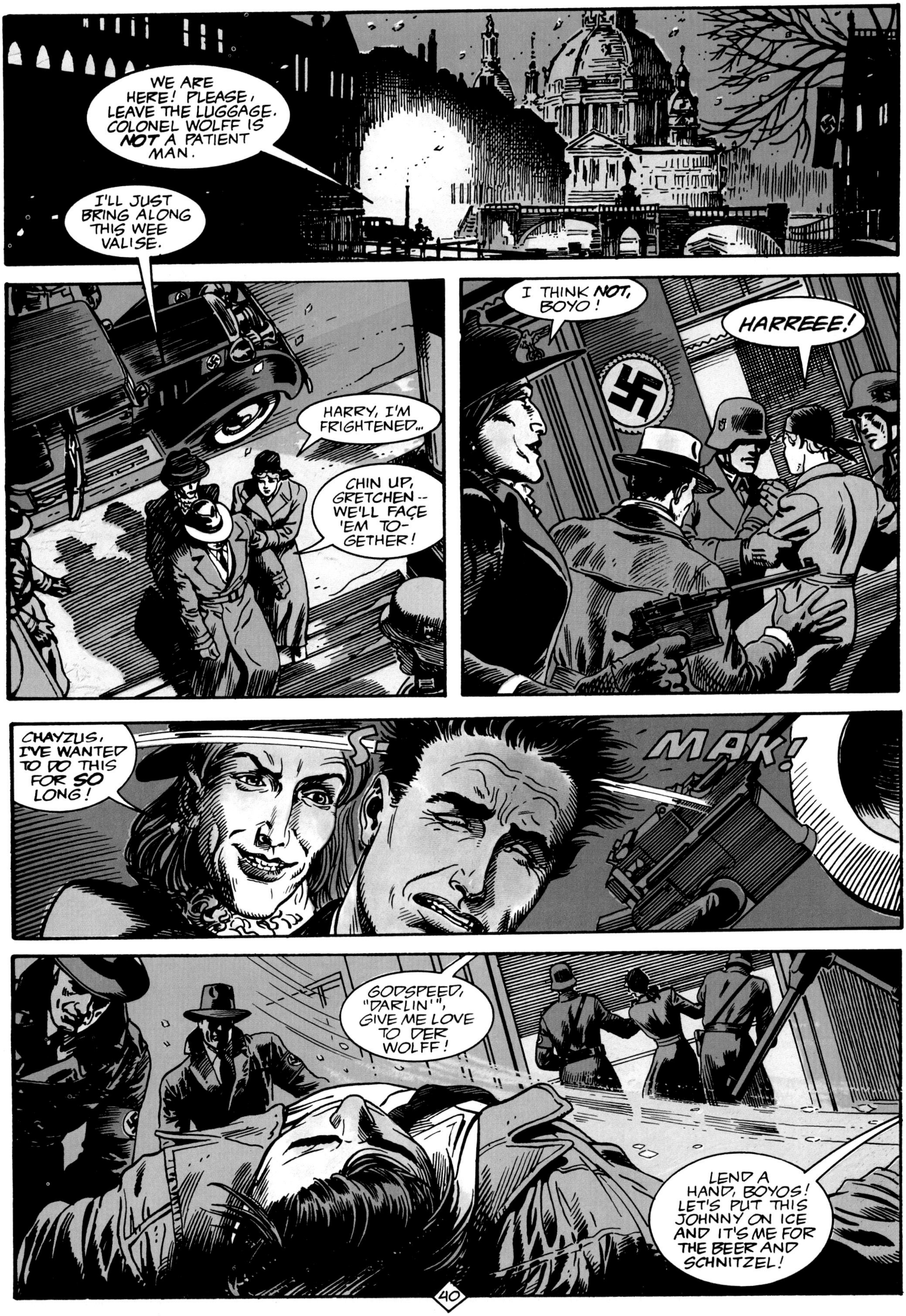
WE ARE HERE! PLEASE, LEAVE THE LUGGAGE. COLONEL WOLFF IS NOT A PATIENT MAN.
I'LL JUST BRING ALONG THIS WEE VALISE.
HARRY, I'M FRIGHTENED...
CHIN UP, GRETCHEN -- WE'LL FACE 'EM TOGETHER!
I THINK NOT, BOYO!
HARREEE!
CHAYZUS, I'VE WANTED TO DO THIS FOR SO LONG!
S-MAK!
GODSPEED, "DARLIN'", GIVE ME LOVE TO DER WOLFF!
LEND A HAND, BOYOS! LET'S PUT THIS JOHNNY ON ICE AND IT'S ME FOR THE BEER AND SCHNITZEL!

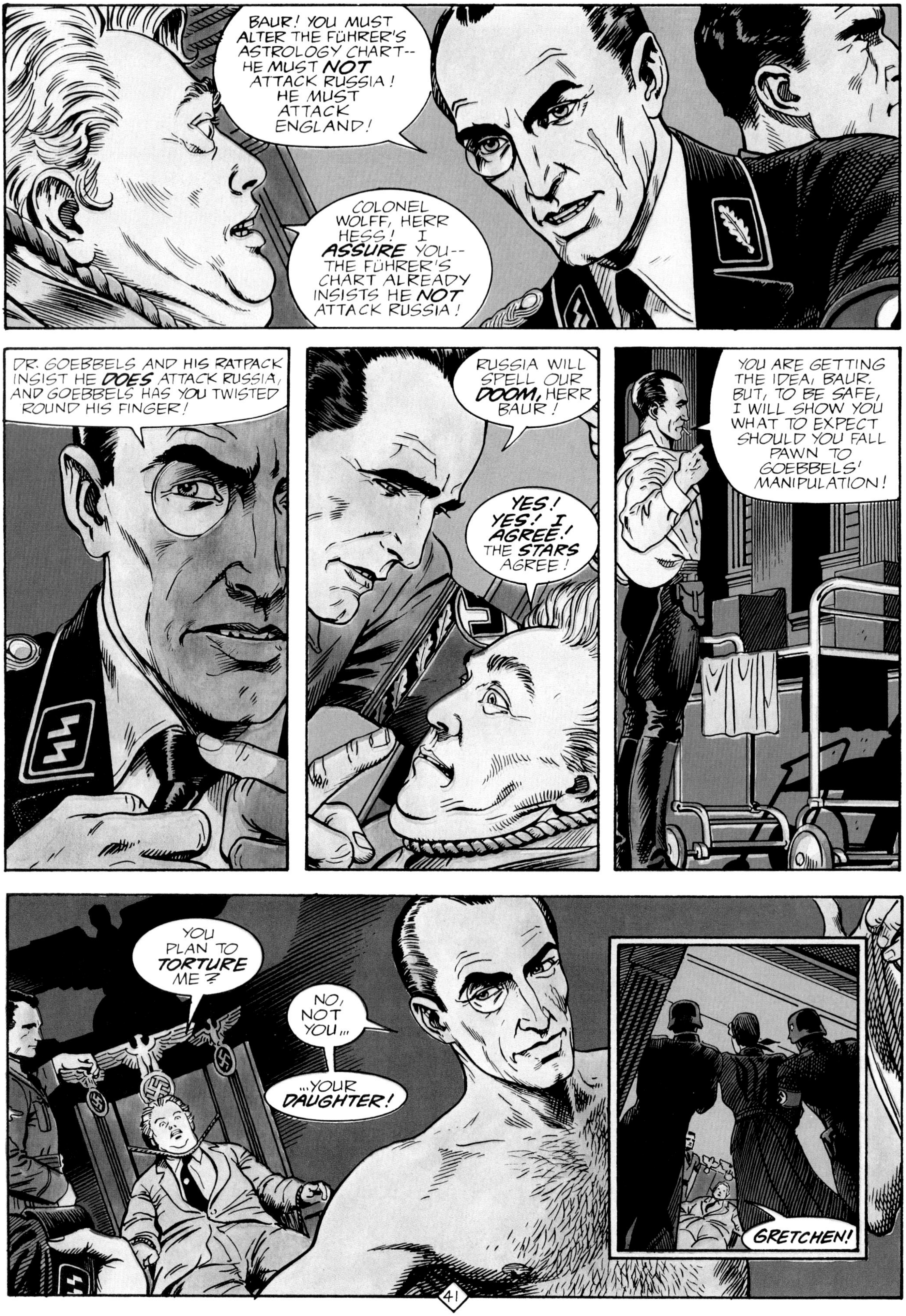
BAUR! YOU MUST ALTER THE FÜHRER'S ASTROLOGY CHART-- HE MUST NOT ATTACK RUSSIA! HE MUST ATTACK ENGLAND!
COLONEL WOLFF, HERR HESS! I ASSURE YOU-- THE FÜHRER'S CHART ALREADY INSISTS HE NOT ATTACK RUSSIA!
DR. GOEBBELS AND HIS RATPACK INSIST HE DOES ATTACK RUSSIA, AND GOEBBELS HAS YOU TWISTED ROUND HIS FINGER!
RUSSIA WILL SPELL OUR DOOM, HERR BAUR!
YES! YES! I AGREE! THE STARS AGREE!
YOU ARE GETTING THE IDEA, BAUR. BUT, TO BE SAFE, I WILL SHOW YOU WHAT TO EXPECT SHOULD YOU FALL PAWN TO GOEBBELS' MANIPULATION!
YOU PLAN TO TORTURE ME?
NO, NOT YOU...
...YOUR DAUGHTER!
GRETCHEN!

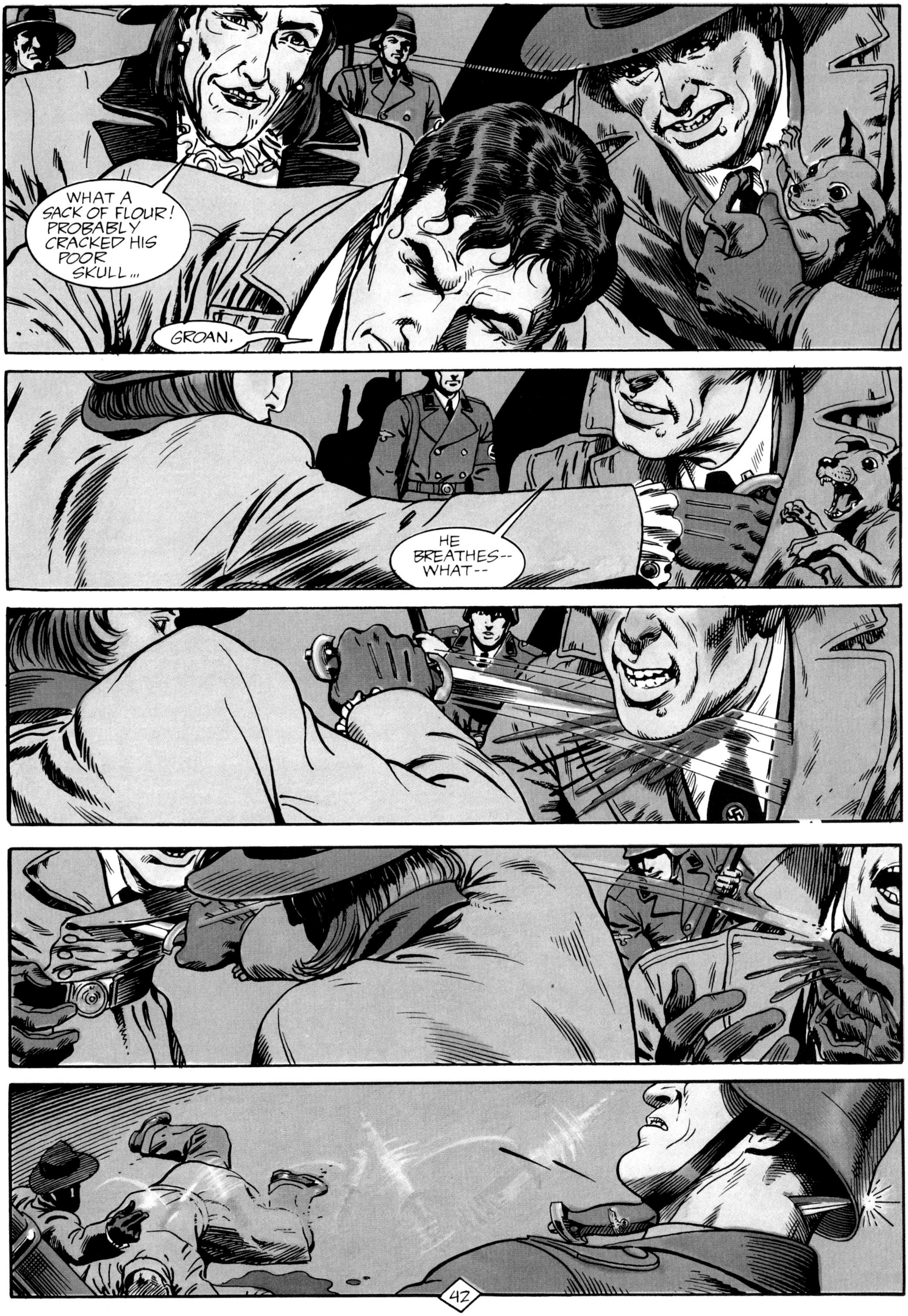
WHAT A SACK OF FLOUR! PROBABLY CRACKED HIS POOR SKULL...
GROAN.
HE BREATHES-- WHAT--

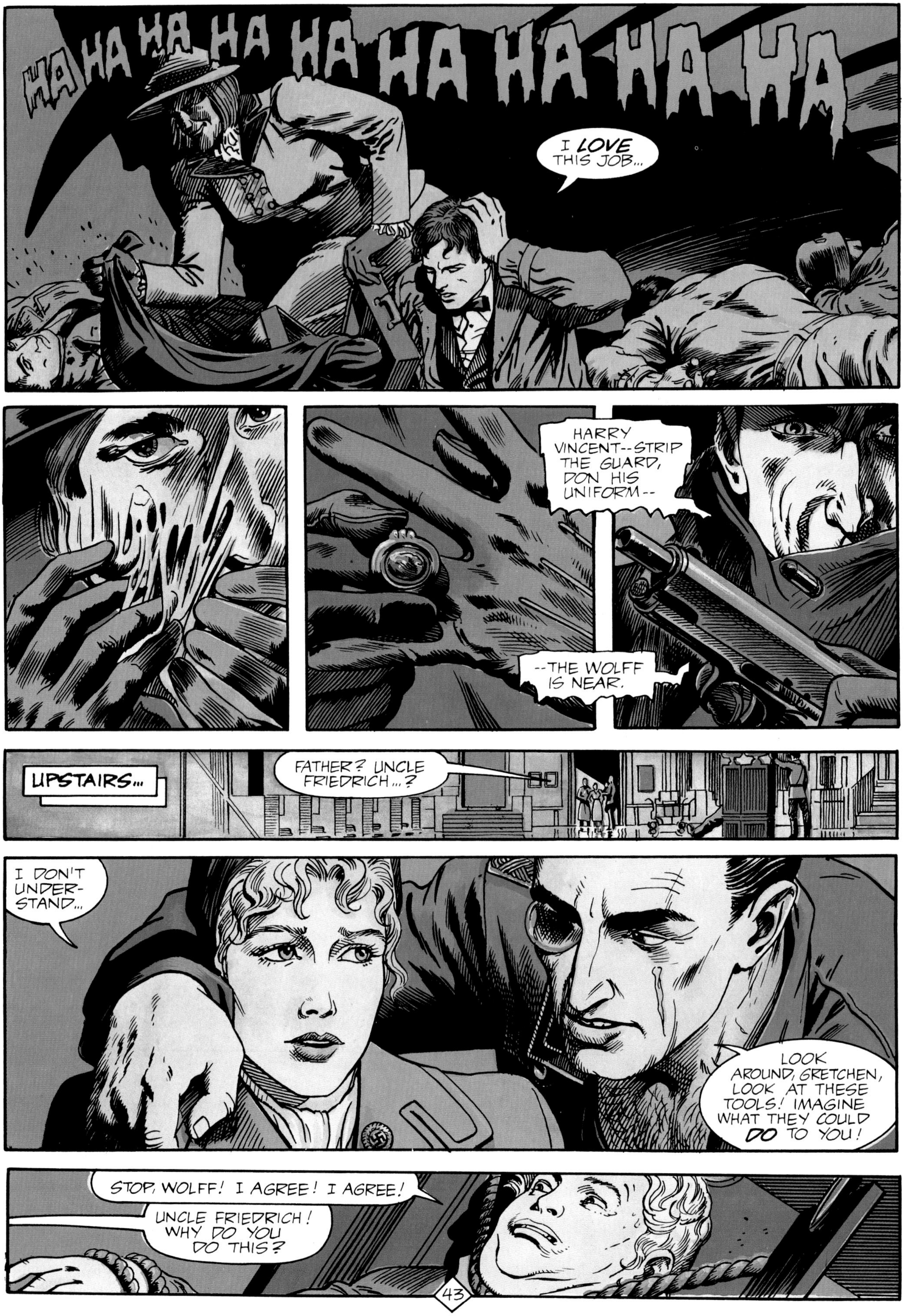
HA HA HA HA HA HA HA HA HA HA HA HA
I LOVE THIS JOB...
HARRY VINCENT--STRIP THE GUARD, DON HIS UNIFORM--
--THE WOLFF IS NEAR.
UPSTAIRS...
FATHER? UNCLE FRIEDRICH...?
I DON'T UNDER-STAND...
LOOK AROUND, GRETCHEN, LOOK AT THESE TOOLS! IMAGINE WHAT THEY COULD DO TO YOU!
STOP, WOLFF! I AGREE! I AGREE!
UNCLE FRIEDRICH! WHY DO YOU DO THIS?

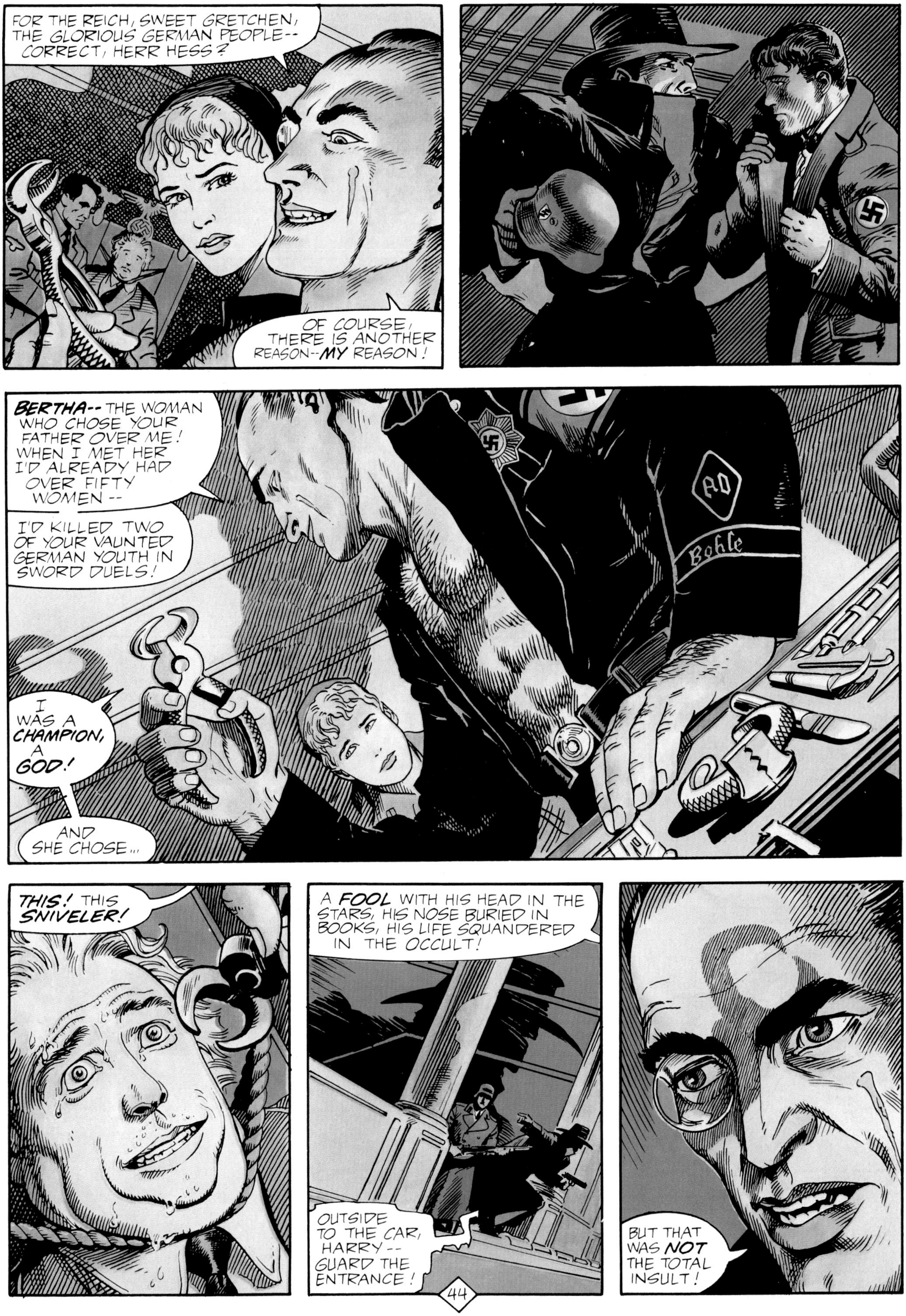
FOR THE REICH, SWEET GRETCHEN, THE GLORIOUS GERMAN PEOPLE-- CORRECT, HERR HESS?
OF COURSE, THERE IS ANOTHER REASON--MY REASON!
BERTHA-- THE WOMAN WHO CHOSE YOUR FATHER OVER ME! WHEN I MET HER I'D ALREADY HAD OVER FIFTY WOMEN --
I'D KILLED TWO OF YOUR VAUNTED GERMAN YOUTH IN SWORD DUELS!
I WAS A CHAMPION, A GOD!
AND SHE CHOSE...
THIS! THIS SNIVELER!
A FOOL WITH HIS HEAD IN THE STARS, HIS NOSE BURIED IN BOOKS, HIS LIFE SQUANDERED IN THE OCCULT!
OUTSIDE TO THE CAR, HARRY -- GUARD THE ENTRANCE!
BUT THAT WAS NOT THE TOTAL INSULT!

FIVE YEARS AGO, WHEN HER ANCESTRY WAS DISCOVERED -- HER TAINTED BLOOD -- YOU *GAVE* HER TO ME --

-- VOLUNTARILY!

YOU WOULDN'T FIGHT FOR HER -- JUST THREW HER AWAY LIKE THE GARBAGE YOU HAD MADE HER!

COLONEL WOLFF, IS THIS NECESSARY?

UNDER THESE HANDS SHE PAID FOR HER INSULT TO ME. AND UNDER THESE HANDS YOU WILL PAY IN THE ONLY COIN YOU COULD CARE ABOUT!

BELIEVE ME, BAUR, IT WOULD BE *YOUR* SKIN THAT WOULD FEEL MY BLADE IF YOUR DAMN CRAFT WERE NOT SO NECESSARY TO MY PLANS.

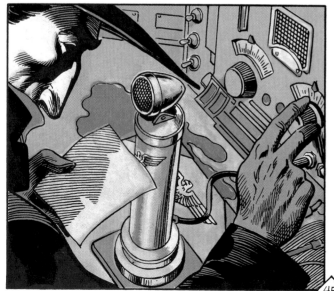

WATCH NOW AS YOUR GRETCHEN PAYS THE DOUBLE PRICE YOU'VE EARNED!

DEUTSCHE Grammophon Gesellschaft
RICHARD WAGNER
GÖTTERDÄMMERUNG
VON KARAJAN

45

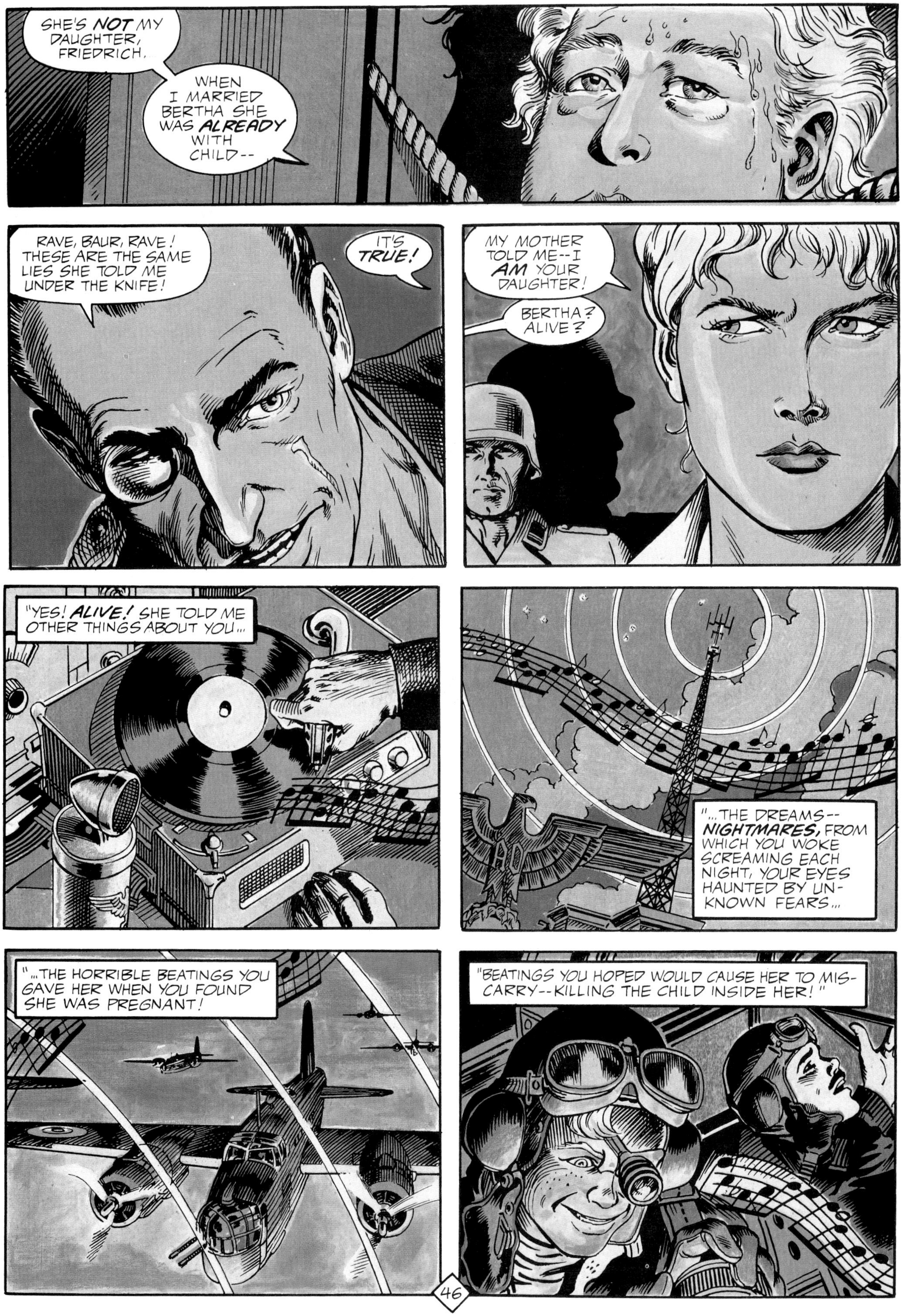
SHE'S NOT MY DAUGHTER, FRIEDRICH...
WHEN I MARRIED BERTHA SHE WAS ALREADY WITH CHILD--
RAVE, BAUR, RAVE! THESE ARE THE SAME LIES SHE TOLD ME UNDER THE KNIFE!
IT'S TRUE!
MY MOTHER TOLD ME--I AM YOUR DAUGHTER!
BERTHA? ALIVE?
"YES! ALIVE! SHE TOLD ME OTHER THINGS ABOUT YOU...
"...THE DREAMS--NIGHTMARES, FROM WHICH YOU WOKE SCREAMING EACH NIGHT, YOUR EYES HAUNTED BY UN-KNOWN FEARS...
"...THE HORRIBLE BEATINGS YOU GAVE HER WHEN YOU FOUND SHE WAS PREGNANT!
"BEATINGS YOU HOPED WOULD CAUSE HER TO MIS-CARRY--KILLING THE CHILD INSIDE HER!"

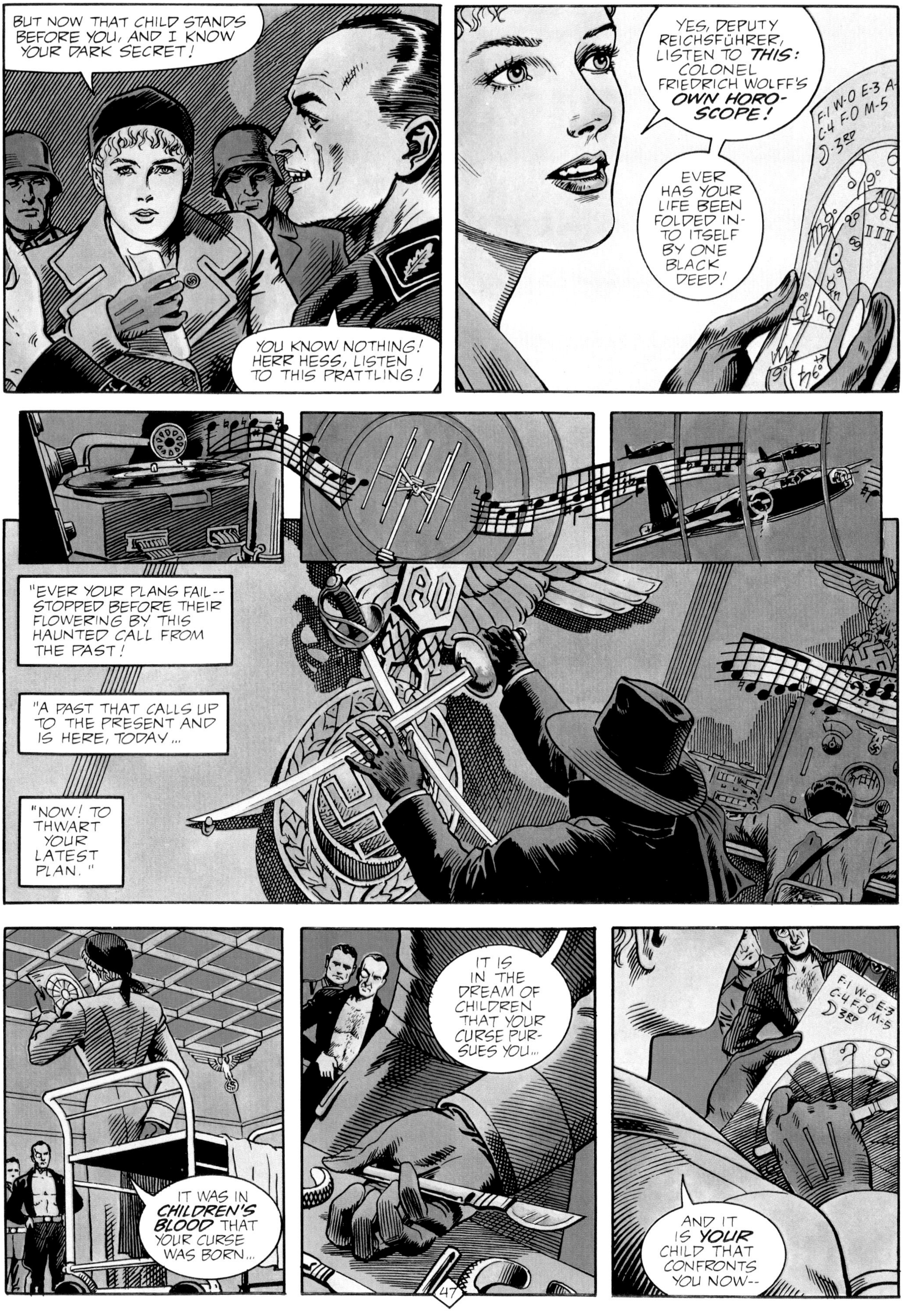

BUT NOW THAT CHILD STANDS BEFORE YOU, AND I KNOW YOUR DARK SECRET!
YOU KNOW NOTHING! HERR HESS, LISTEN TO THIS PRATTLING!
YES, DEPUTY REICHSFÜHRER, LISTEN TO **THIS:** COLONEL FRIEDRICH WOLFF'S **OWN HORO-SCOPE!**
EVER HAS YOUR LIFE BEEN FOLDED IN-TO ITSELF BY ONE BLACK DEED!
"EVER YOUR PLANS FAIL-- STOPPED BEFORE THEIR FLOWERING BY THIS HAUNTED CALL FROM THE PAST!
"A PAST THAT CALLS UP TO THE PRESENT AND IS HERE, TODAY...
"NOW! TO THWART YOUR LATEST PLAN."
IT WAS IN **CHILDREN'S BLOOD** THAT YOUR CURSE WAS BORN...
IT IS IN THE DREAM OF CHILDREN THAT YOUR CURSE PUR-SUES YOU...
F-1 W-0 E-3
C-4 F-0 M-5
AND IT IS **YOUR** CHILD THAT CONFRONTS YOU NOW--

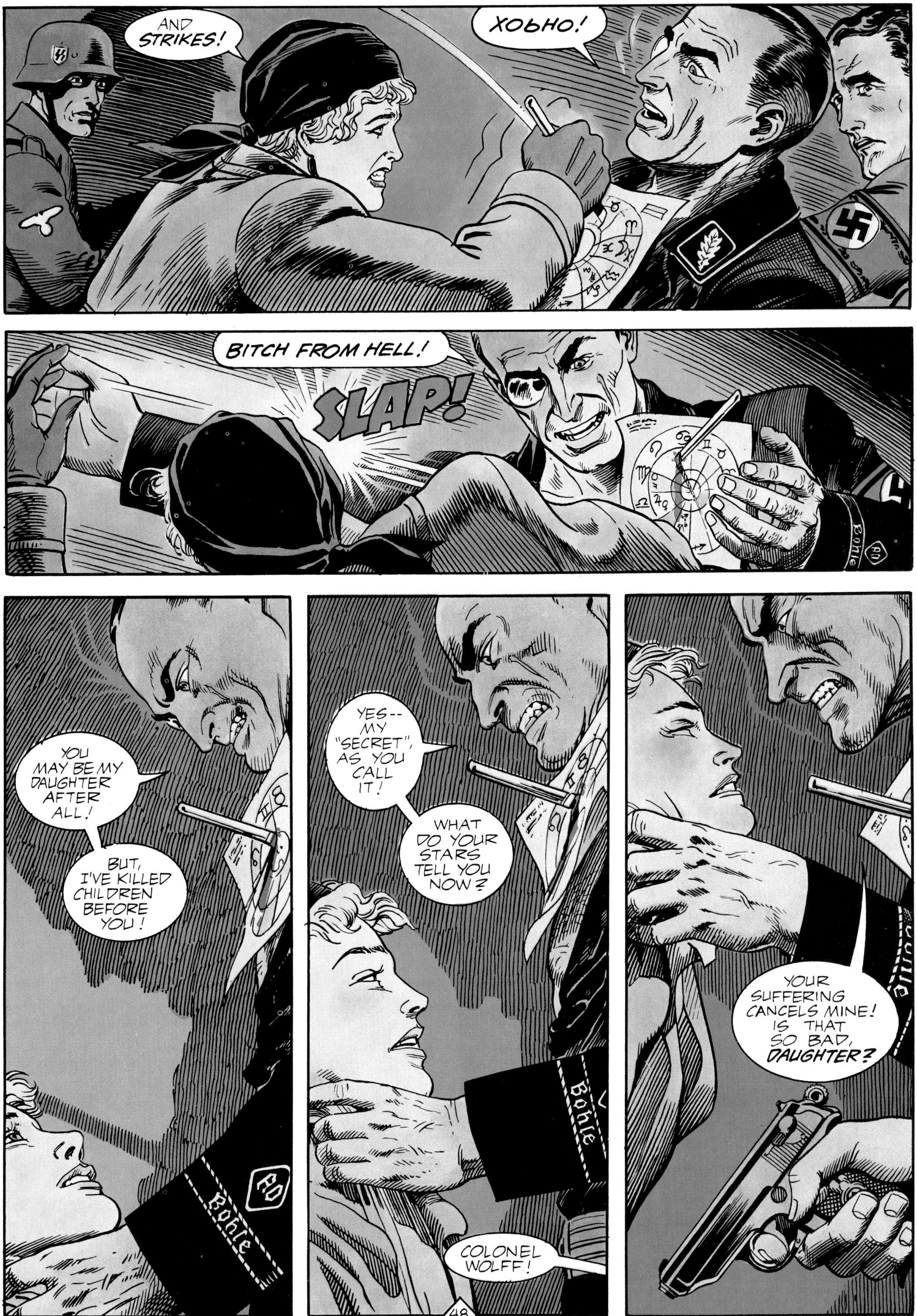
AND STRIKES!
ХОЬНО!
BITCH FROM HELL!
SLAP!
YOU MAY BE MY DAUGHTER AFTER ALL!
BUT, I'VE KILLED CHILDREN BEFORE YOU!
YES-- MY "SECRET", AS YOU CALL IT!
WHAT DO YOUR STARS TELL YOU NOW?
COLONEL WOLFF!
YOUR SUFFERING CANCELS MINE! IS THAT SO BAD, DAUGHTER?

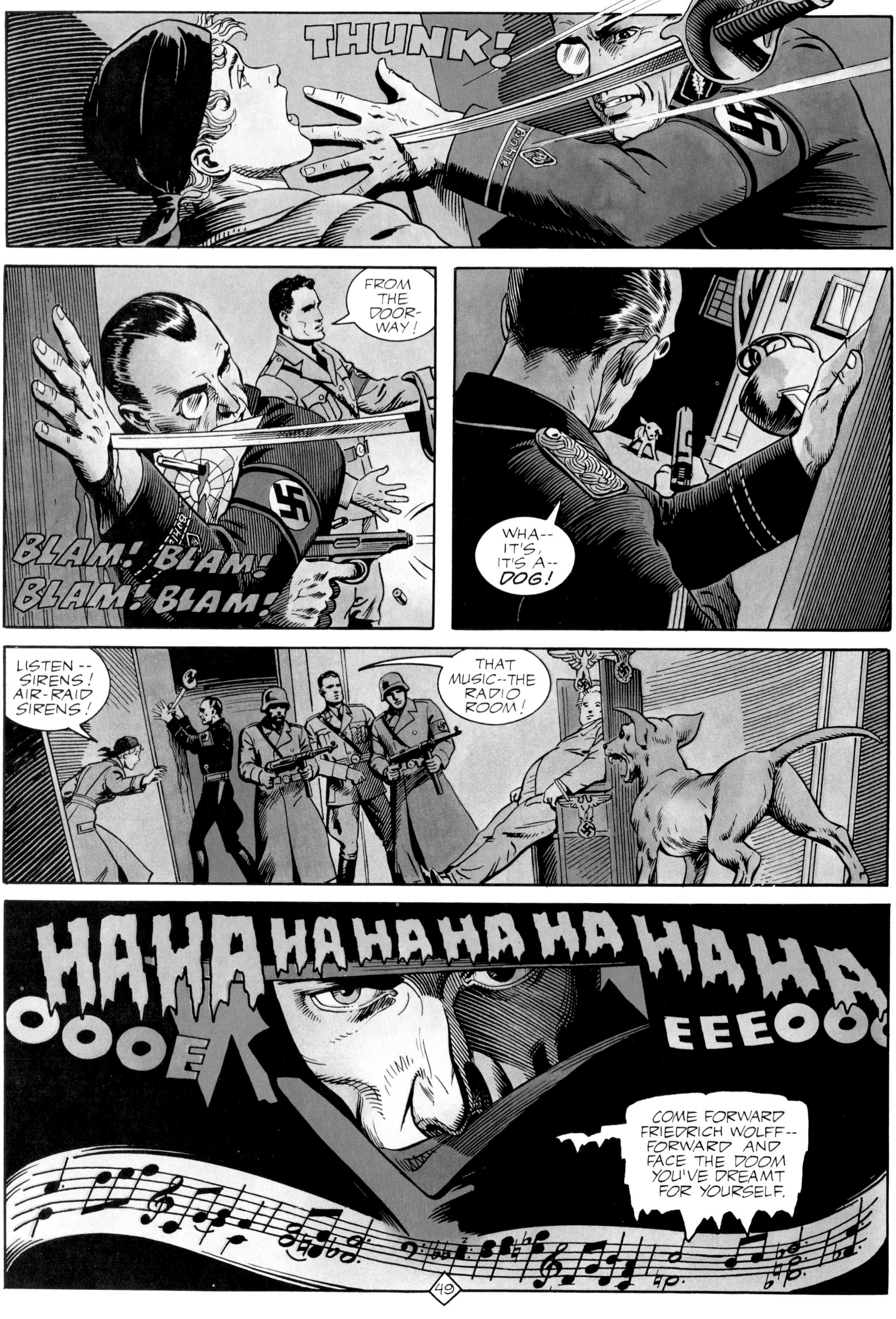
THUNK!
FROM THE DOOR-WAY!
BLAM! BLAM! BLAM! BLAM!
WHA-- IT'S, IT'S A-- DOG!
LISTEN -- SIRENS! AIR-RAID SIRENS!
THAT MUSIC--THE RADIO ROOM!
HA-HA HAHAHAHAHAHA HAHA
OOOE EEEOO
COME FORWARD FRIEDRICH WOLFF-- FORWARD AND FACE THE DOOM YOU'VE DREAMT FOR YOURSELF.

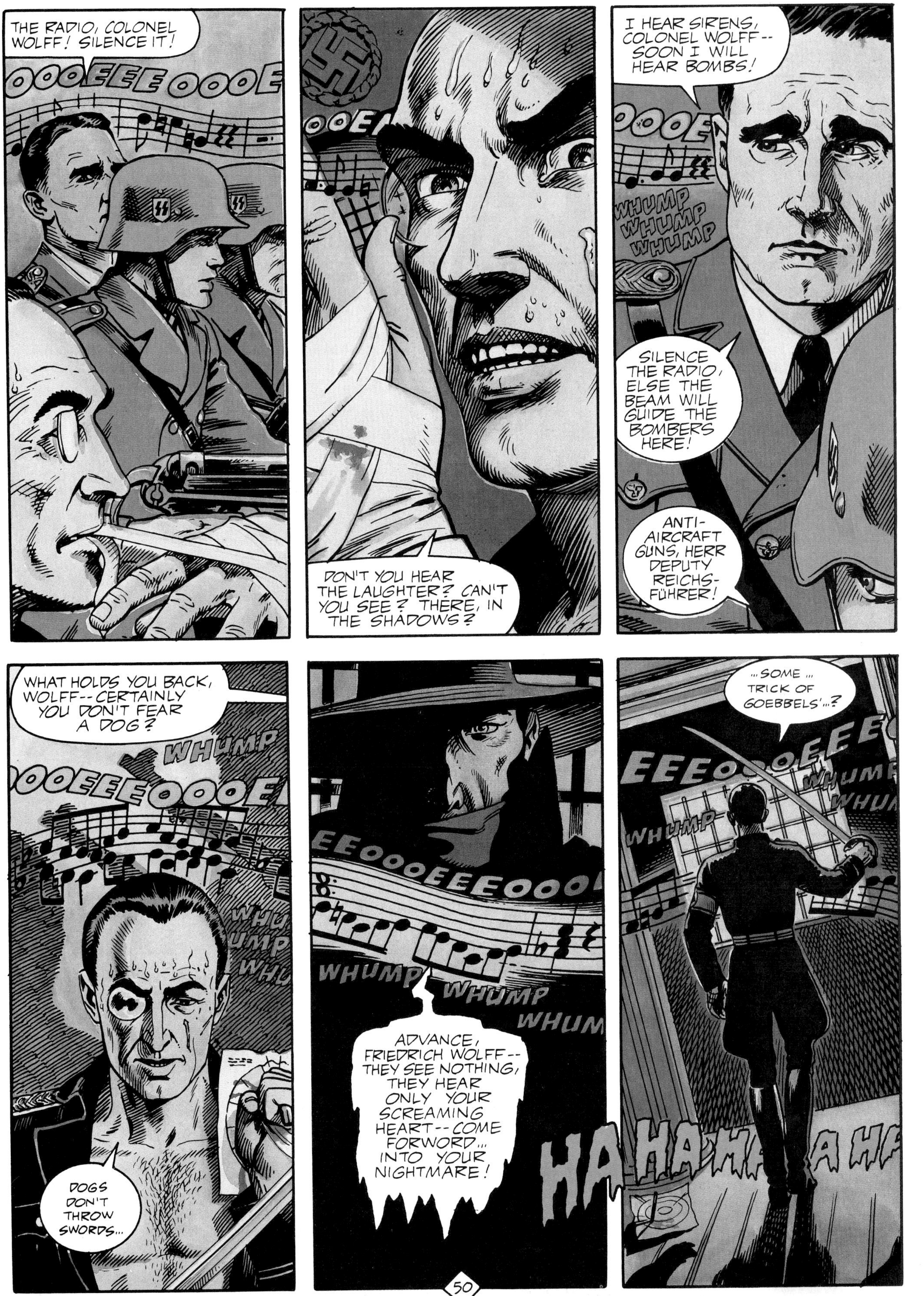
THE RADIO, COLONEL WOLFF! SILENCE IT!
OOOEEEOOOE
OOOE
DON'T YOU HEAR THE LAUGHTER? CAN'T YOU SEE? THERE, IN THE SHADOWS?
I HEAR SIRENS, COLONEL WOLFF-- SOON I WILL HEAR BOMBS!
OOOE
WHUMP WHUMP WHUMP
SILENCE THE RADIO, ELSE THE BEAM WILL GUIDE THE BOMBERS HERE!
ANTI-AIRCRAFT GUNS, HERR DEPUTY REICHS-FÜHRER!
WHAT HOLDS YOU BACK, WOLFF--CERTAINLY YOU DON'T FEAR A DOG?
WHUMP
OOOEEEOOOE
DOGS DON'T THROW SWORDS...
EEEOOOOEEEOOOO
WHUMP WHUMP WHUM
ADVANCE, FRIEDRICH WOLFF-- THEY SEE NOTHING, THEY HEAR ONLY YOUR SCREAMING HEART--COME FORWORD... INTO YOUR NIGHTMARE!
...SOME ... TRICK OF GOEBBELS'...?
EEEOOOEEE
WHUMP
HA HA HA HA HA

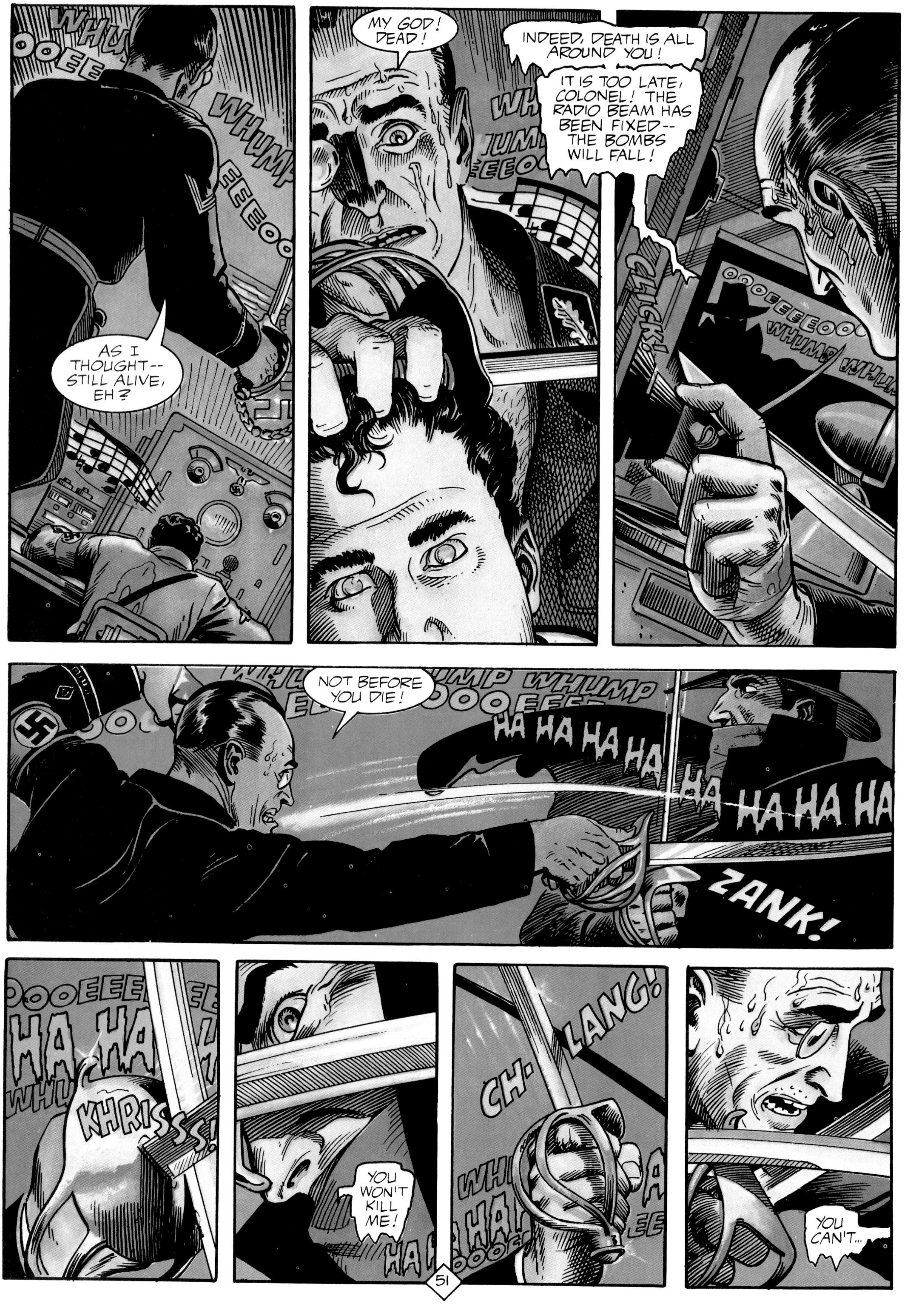
WHUM
OOEEE
WHUMP
EEEOO
AS I THOUGHT-- STILL ALIVE, EH?
MY GOD! DEAD!
INDEED, DEATH IS ALL AROUND YOU!
IT IS TOO LATE, COLONEL! THE RADIO BEAM HAS BEEN FIXED-- THE BOMBS WILL FALL!
CLICK!
OOEEEEEOO
WHUMP
NOT BEFORE YOU DIE!
WHUMP WHUMP
HA HA HA HA HA HA HA HA HA HA
ZANK!
OOOEEEEE
HA HA
KHRISSS!
YOU WON'T KILL ME!
CH- LANG!
YOU CAN'T...

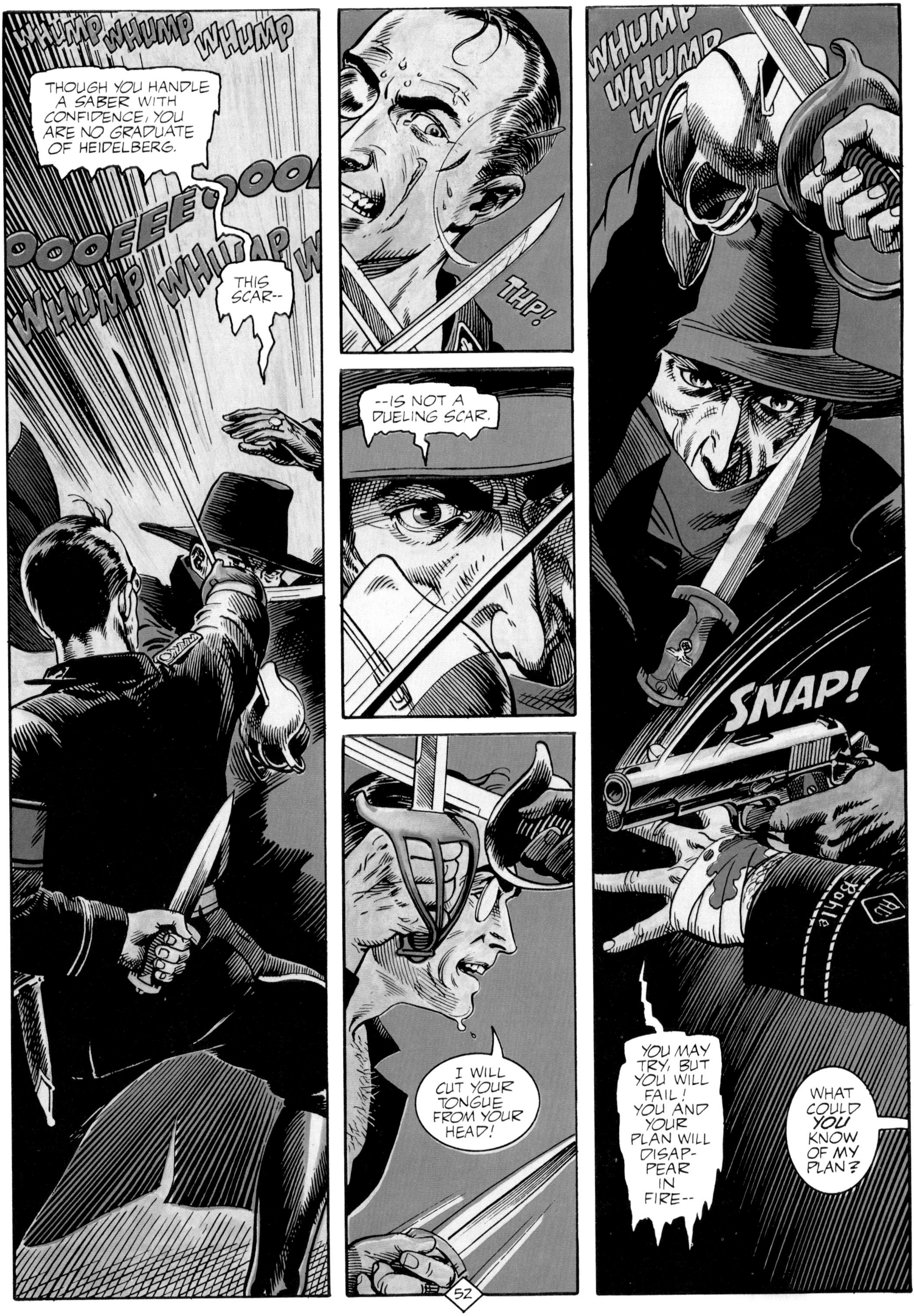
WHUMP WHUMP WHUMP
THOUGH YOU HANDLE A SABER WITH CONFIDENCE, YOU ARE NO GRADUATE OF HEIDELBERG.
OOOEEEOOOO
WHUMP WHUMP WHUMP
THIS SCAR--
THP!
--IS NOT A DUELING SCAR.
I WILL CUT YOUR TONGUE FROM YOUR HEAD!
WHUMP WHUMP
SNAP!
Rohle
YOU MAY TRY, BUT YOU WILL FAIL! YOU AND YOUR PLAN WILL DISAP-PEAR IN FIRE--
WHAT COULD YOU KNOW OF MY PLAN?

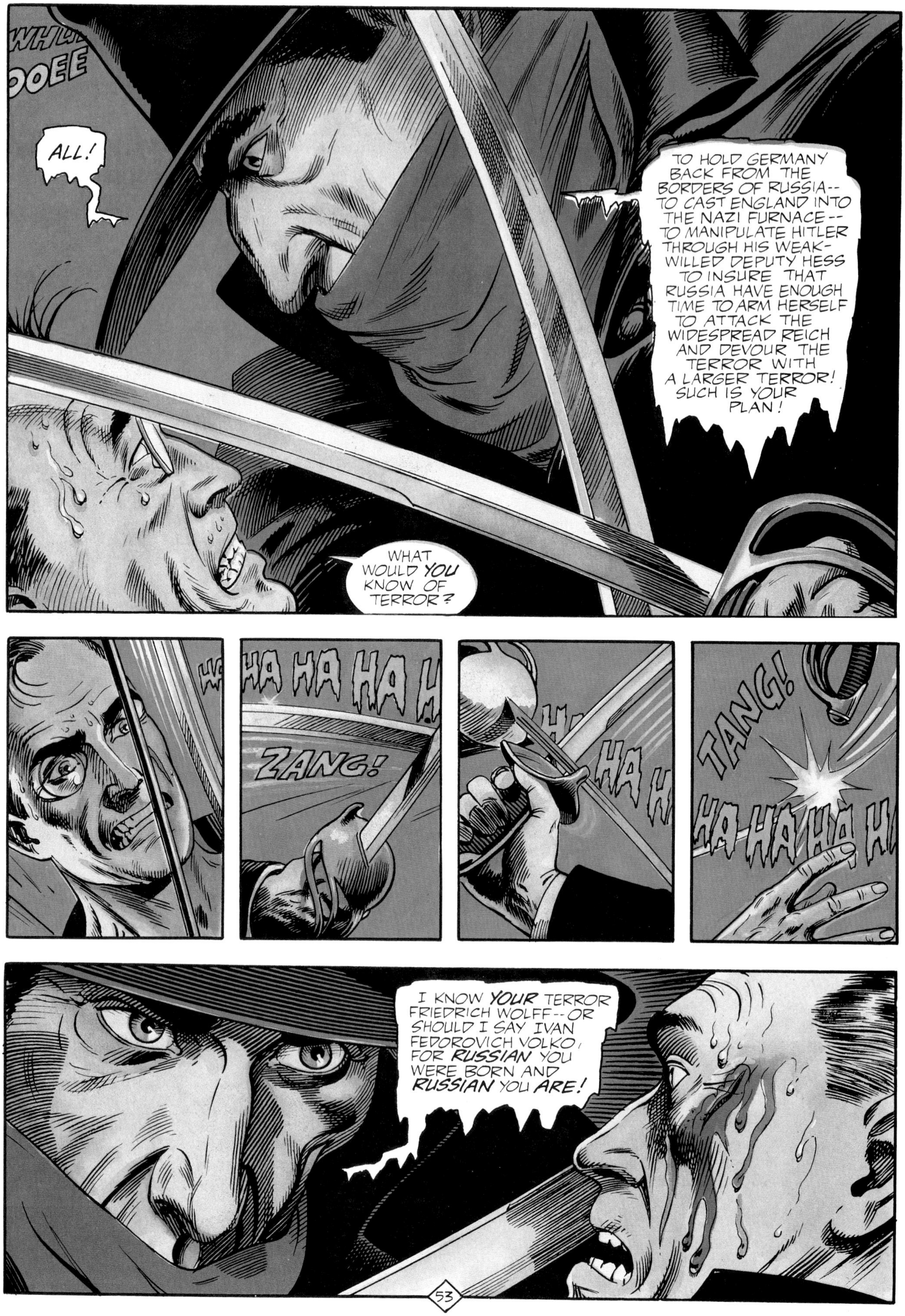
WHUDOEE
ALL!
TO HOLD GERMANY BACK FROM THE BORDERS OF RUSSIA-- TO CAST ENGLAND INTO THE NAZI FURNACE-- TO MANIPULATE HITLER THROUGH HIS WEAK-WILLED DEPUTY HESS TO INSURE THAT RUSSIA HAVE ENOUGH TIME TO ARM HERSELF TO ATTACK THE WIDESPREAD REICH AND DEVOUR THE TERROR WITH A LARGER TERROR! SUCH IS YOUR PLAN!
WHAT WOULD YOU KNOW OF TERROR?
HA HA HA HA
ZANG!
HA HA
TANG!
HA HA HA HA
I KNOW YOUR TERROR FRIEDRICH WOLFF--OR SHOULD I SAY IVAN FEDOROVICH VOLKO, FOR RUSSIAN YOU WERE BORN AND RUSSIAN YOU ARE!

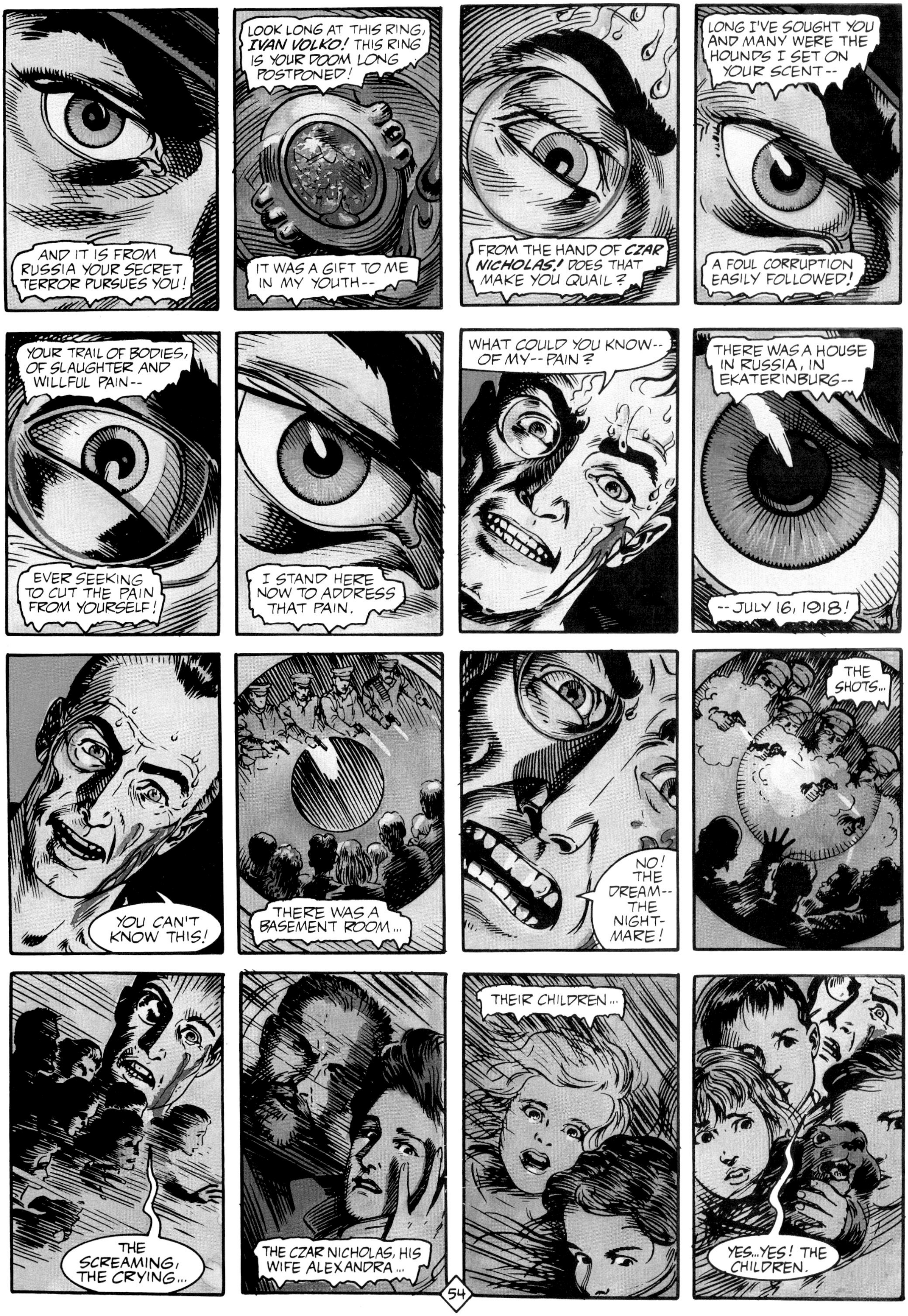
AND IT IS FROM RUSSIA YOUR SECRET TERROR PURSUES YOU!
LOOK LONG AT THIS RING, IVAN VOLKO! THIS RING IS YOUR DOOM LONG POSTPONED!
IT WAS A GIFT TO ME IN MY YOUTH--
FROM THE HAND OF CZAR NICHOLAS! DOES THAT MAKE YOU QUAIL?
LONG I'VE SOUGHT YOU AND MANY WERE THE HOUNDS I SET ON YOUR SCENT--
A FOUL CORRUPTION EASILY FOLLOWED!
YOUR TRAIL OF BODIES, OF SLAUGHTER AND WILLFUL PAIN--
EVER SEEKING TO CUT THE PAIN FROM YOURSELF!
I STAND HERE NOW TO ADDRESS THAT PAIN.
WHAT COULD YOU KNOW--OF MY--PAIN?
THERE WAS A HOUSE IN RUSSIA, IN EKATERINBURG--
--JULY 16, 1918!
YOU CAN'T KNOW THIS!
THERE WAS A BASEMENT ROOM...
NO! THE DREAM--THE NIGHT-MARE!
THE SHOTS...
THE SCREAMING, THE CRYING...
THE CZAR NICHOLAS, HIS WIFE ALEXANDRA...
THEIR CHILDREN...
YES...YES! THE CHILDREN.

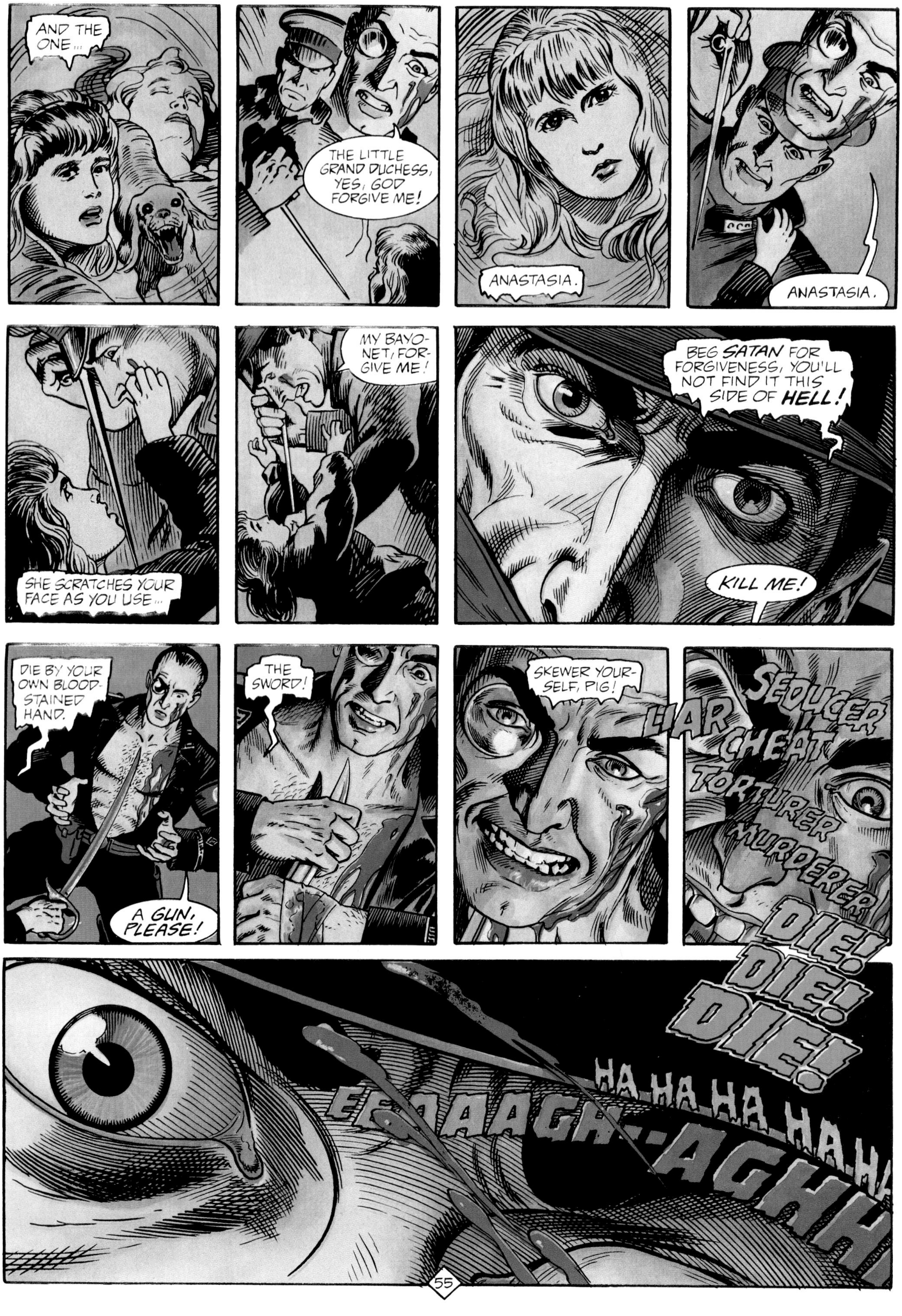
AND THE ONE...
THE LITTLE GRAND DUCHESS, YES, GOD FORGIVE ME!
ANASTASIA.
ANASTASIA.
SHE SCRATCHES YOUR FACE AS YOU USE...
MY BAYONET, FORGIVE ME!
BEG SATAN FOR FORGIVENESS, YOU'LL NOT FIND IT THIS SIDE OF HELL!
KILL ME!
DIE BY YOUR OWN BLOOD-STAINED HAND.
A GUN, PLEASE!
THE SWORD!
SKEWER YOURSELF, PIG!
SEDUCER
LIAR
CHEAT
TORTURER
MURDERER
DIE! DIE! DIE!
HA HA HA HA HA HA
EEAAAAGH--AGHH

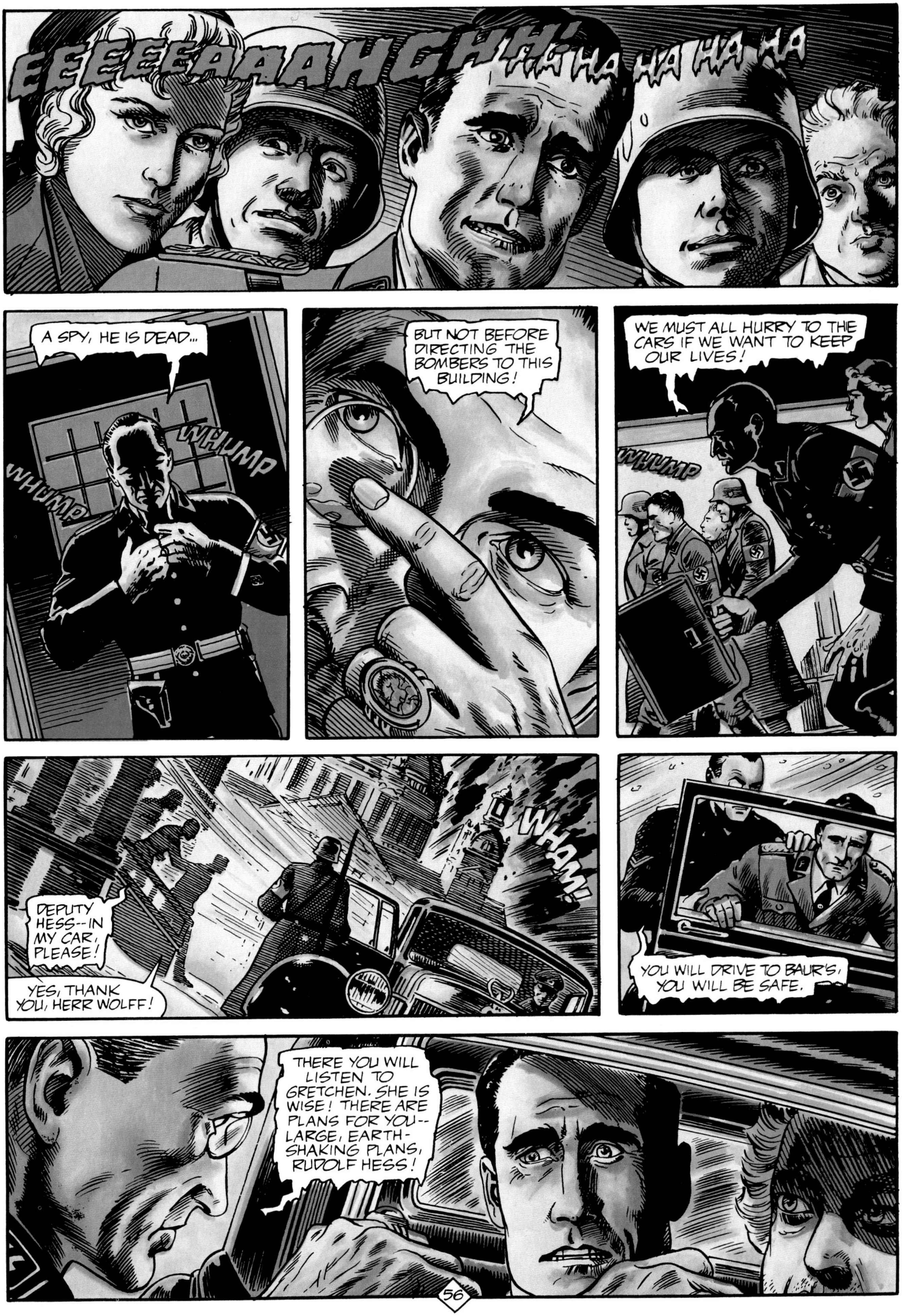
EEEEEAAAHGHH! HA HA HA HA HA
A SPY, HE IS DEAD...
WHUMP
WHUMP
BUT NOT BEFORE DIRECTING THE BOMBERS TO THIS BUILDING!
WE MUST ALL HURRY TO THE CARS IF WE WANT TO KEEP OUR LIVES!
WHUMP
WHAM!
DEPUTY HESS--IN MY CAR, PLEASE!
YES, THANK YOU, HERR WOLFF!
YOU WILL DRIVE TO BAUR'S. YOU WILL BE SAFE.
THERE YOU WILL LISTEN TO GRETCHEN. SHE IS WISE! THERE ARE PLANS FOR YOU-- LARGE, EARTH-SHAKING PLANS, RUDOLF HESS!

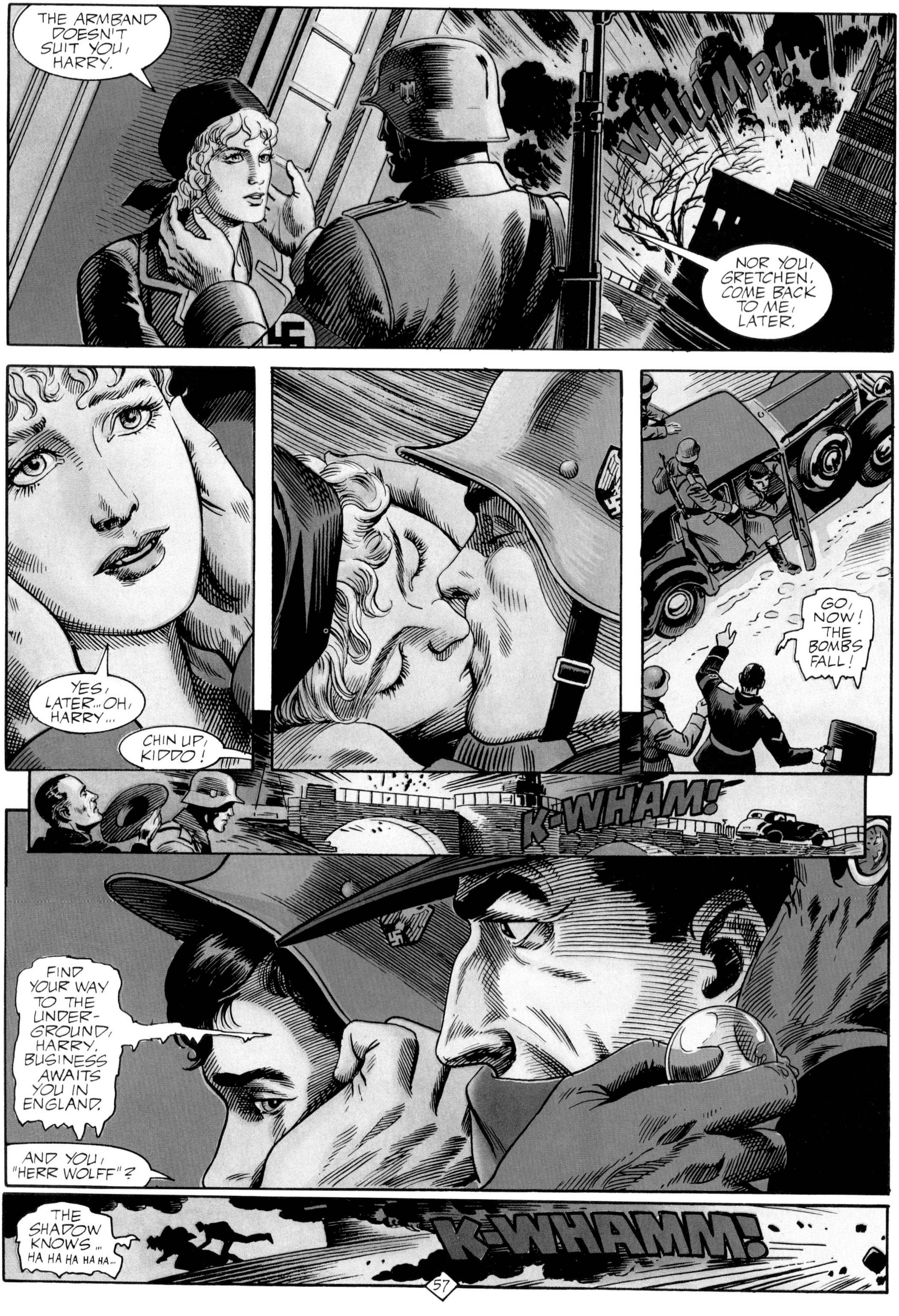
THE ARMBAND DOESN'T SUIT YOU, HARRY.
WHUMP!
NOR YOU, GRETCHEN. COME BACK TO ME, LATER.
YES, LATER...OH, HARRY...
CHIN UP, KIDDO!
GO, NOW! THE BOMBS FALL!
K-WHAM!
FIND YOUR WAY TO THE UNDERGROUND, HARRY. BUSINESS AWAITS YOU IN ENGLAND.
AND YOU, "HERR WOLFF"?
THE SHADOW KNOWS... HA HA HA HA HA...
K-WHAMM!

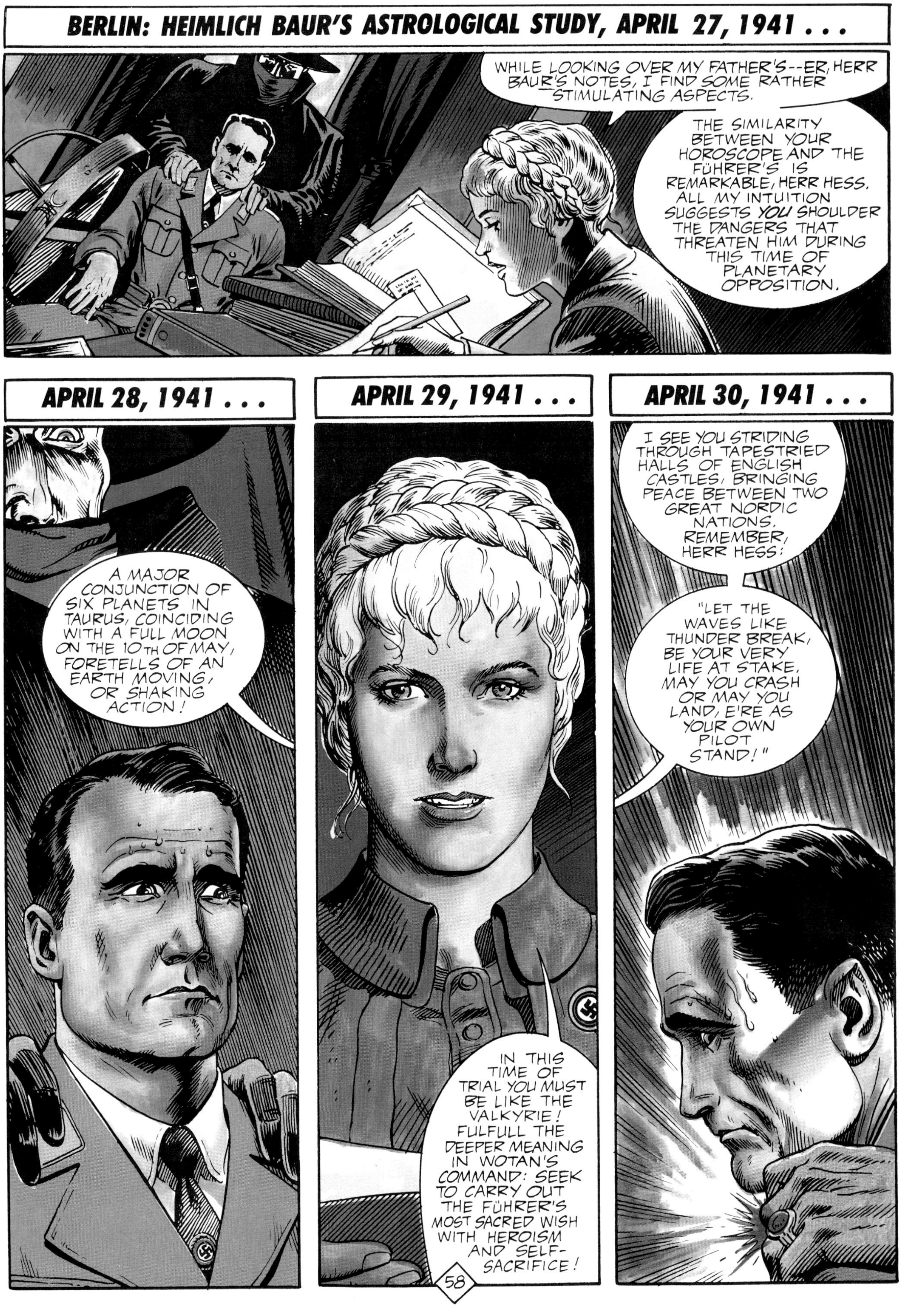
BERLIN: HEIMLICH BAUR'S ASTROLOGICAL STUDY, APRIL 27, 1941 . . .
WHILE LOOKING OVER MY FATHER'S--ER, HERR BAUR'S NOTES, I FIND SOME RATHER STIMULATING ASPECTS.
THE SIMILARITY BETWEEN YOUR HOROSCOPE AND THE FÜHRER'S IS REMARKABLE, HERR HESS. ALL MY INTUITION SUGGESTS YOU SHOULDER THE DANGERS THAT THREATEN HIM DURING THIS TIME OF PLANETARY OPPOSITION.
APRIL 28, 1941 . . .
A MAJOR CONJUNCTION OF SIX PLANETS IN TAURUS, COINCIDING WITH A FULL MOON ON THE 10TH OF MAY, FORETELLS OF AN EARTH MOVING, OR SHAKING ACTION!
APRIL 29, 1941 . . .
IN THIS TIME OF TRIAL YOU MUST BE LIKE THE VALKYRIE! FULFULL THE DEEPER MEANING IN WOTAN'S COMMAND: SEEK TO CARRY OUT THE FÜHRER'S MOST SACRED WISH WITH HEROISM AND SELF-SACRIFICE!
APRIL 30, 1941 . . .
I SEE YOU STRIDING THROUGH TAPESTRIED HALLS OF ENGLISH CASTLES, BRINGING PEACE BETWEEN TWO GREAT NORDIC NATIONS. REMEMBER, HERR HESS:
"LET THE WAVES LIKE THUNDER BREAK, BE YOUR VERY LIFE AT STAKE, MAY YOU CRASH OR MAY YOU LAND, E'RE AS YOUR OWN PILOT STAND!"

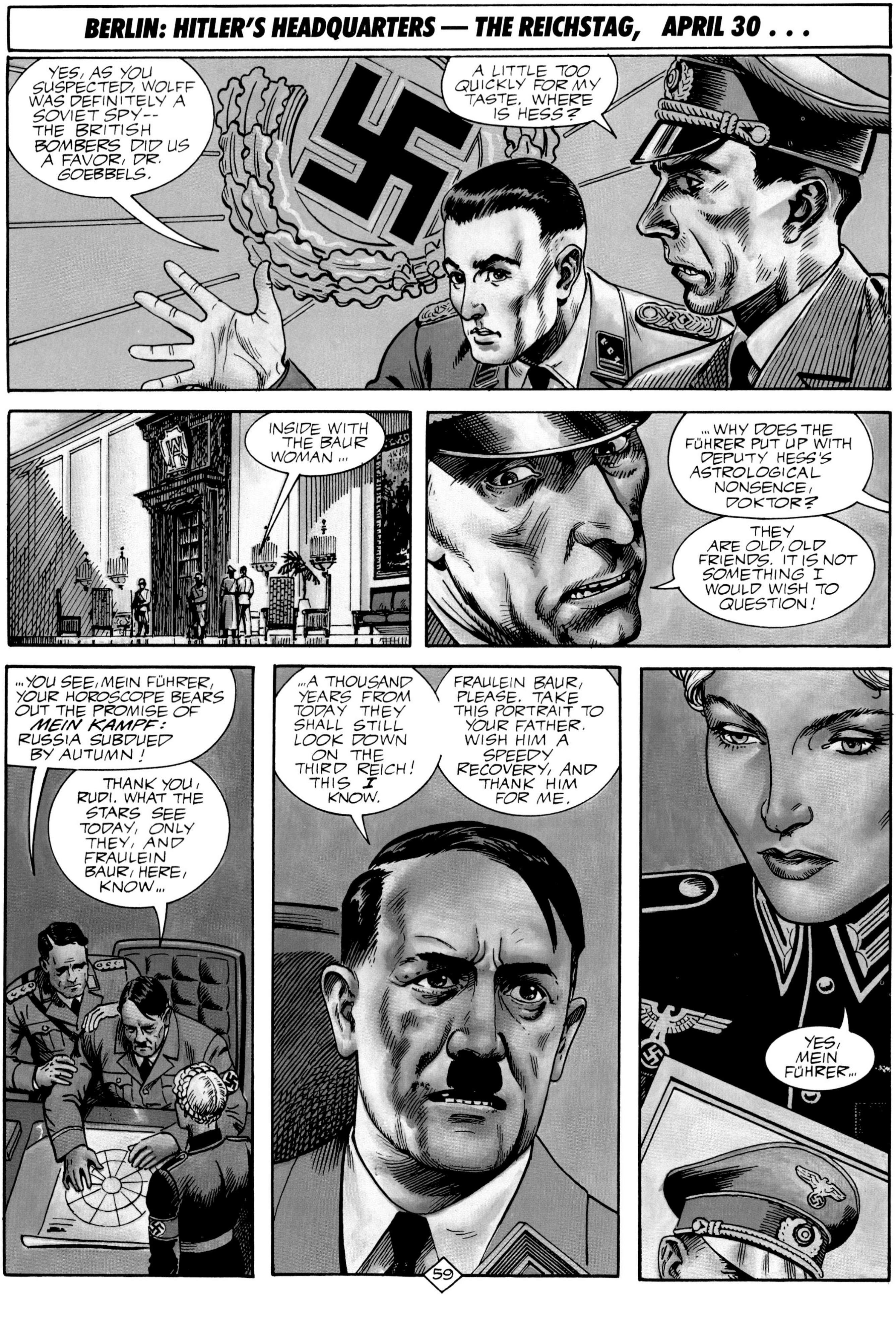
BERLIN: HITLER'S HEADQUARTERS — THE REICHSTAG, APRIL 30 . . .
YES, AS YOU SUSPECTED, WOLFF WAS DEFINITELY A SOVIET SPY-- THE BRITISH BOMBERS DID US A FAVOR, DR. GOEBBELS.
A LITTLE TOO QUICKLY FOR MY TASTE. WHERE IS HESS?
INSIDE WITH THE BAUR WOMAN ...
...WHY DOES THE FÜHRER PUT UP WITH DEPUTY HESS'S ASTROLOGICAL NONSENCE, DOKTOR?
THEY ARE OLD, OLD FRIENDS. IT IS NOT SOMETHING I WOULD WISH TO QUESTION!
...YOU SEE, MEIN FÜHRER, YOUR HOROSCOPE BEARS OUT THE PROMISE OF MEIN KAMPF: RUSSIA SUBDUED BY AUTUMN!
THANK YOU, RUDI. WHAT THE STARS SEE TODAY, ONLY THEY, AND FRAULEIN BAUR, HERE, KNOW...
...A THOUSAND YEARS FROM TODAY THEY SHALL STILL LOOK DOWN ON THE THIRD REICH! THIS I KNOW.
FRAULEIN BAUR, PLEASE. TAKE THIS PORTRAIT TO YOUR FATHER. WISH HIM A SPEEDY RECOVERY, AND THANK HIM FOR ME.
YES, MEIN FÜHRER...

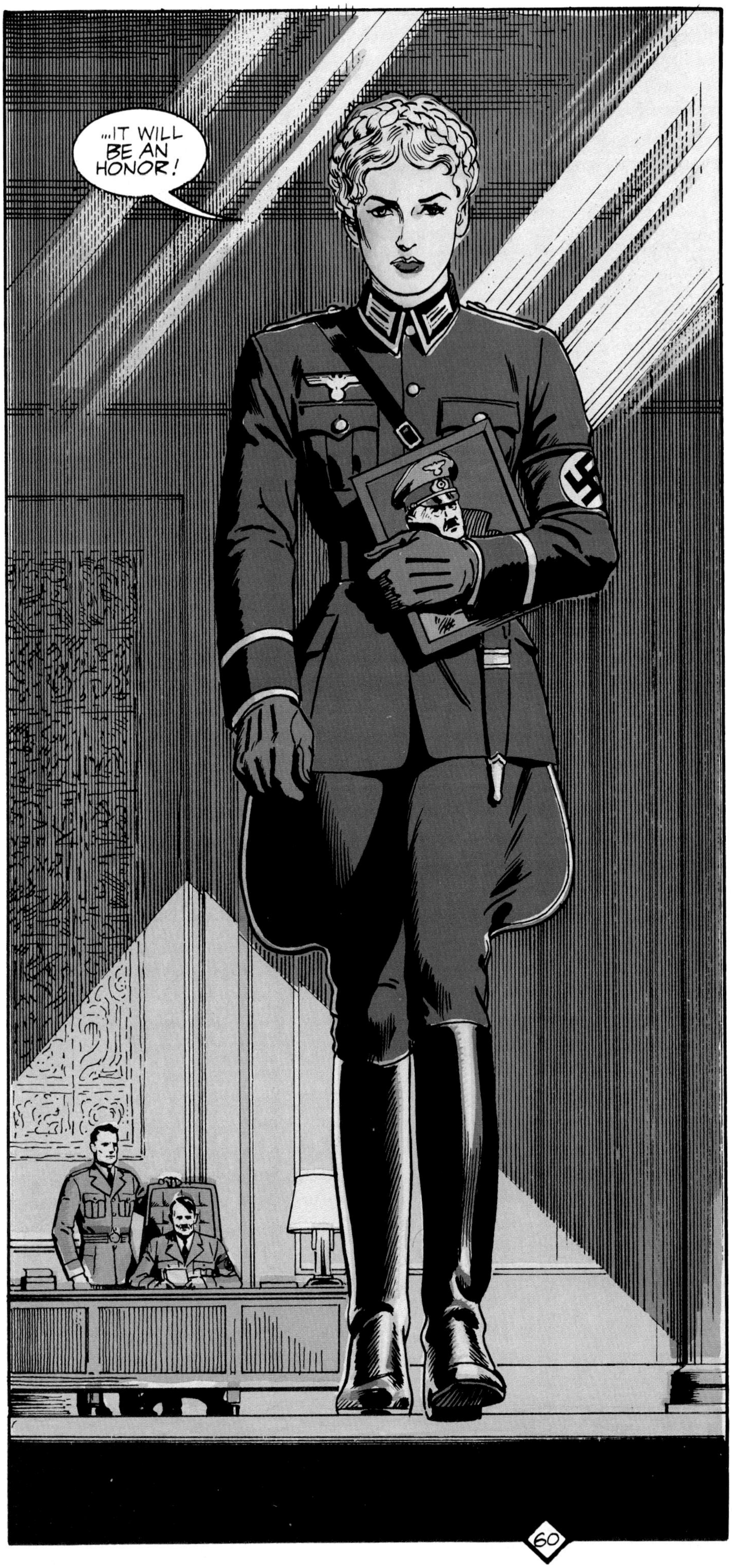
...IT WILL BE AN HONOR!

NINE DAYS LATER, ON MAY 10TH, 1941, UNDER THE MOST BIZARRE CIRCUMSTANCES, DEPUTY REICHSLEITER RUDOLF HESS COMMANDEERED A LONG-RANGE *ME-110* FIGHTER AND FLEW UNERRINGLY TO SCOTLAND.

HE BAILED OUT AND APPROACHED THE BRITISH AUTHORITIES WITH WILD STORIES OF ASTROLOGICALLY PREDICTED VICTORY FOR THE NAZIS AND AN OFFER OF PEACE BETWEEN GERMANY AND BRITAIN.

SINCE HESS WAS DEPUTY REICHSFÜHRER, RUSSIA COULD ONLY ASSUME HIS FLIGHT WAS DIRECTLY ORDERED BY HITLER. FEARING A TRUCE BETWEEN ENGLAND AND GERMANY, STALIN MOBILIZED HIS ARMIES, THEREBY ENSURING THE NAZI ATTACK THAT HAD BEEN FORETOLD BY HITLER'S ASTROLOGER!

ON JUNE 22ND, 1941, HITLER LAUNCHED OPERATION ***BARBARROSA***-- THE MASSIVE INVASION OF THE SOVIET UNION ALONG A THOUSAND MILE FRONT EXTENDING FROM THE BALTIC TO THE BLACK SEA.

ALTHOUGH GERMANY DEPLOYED 3,300 TANKS, 2,770 AIRCRAFT AND MORE THAN 3,300,000 MEN THEY WERE STOPPED 30 MILES FROM MOSCOW, TURNED AT STALINGRAD AND EVENTUALLY FORCED BACK TO THE VERY HEART OF BERLIN.

HISTORIANS DISAGREE AS TO WHY HITLER ATTACKED RUSSIA, BUT MANY THINK HAD HE NOT, GERMANY MAY HAVE EMERGED FROM WORLD WAR II VICTORIOUS.

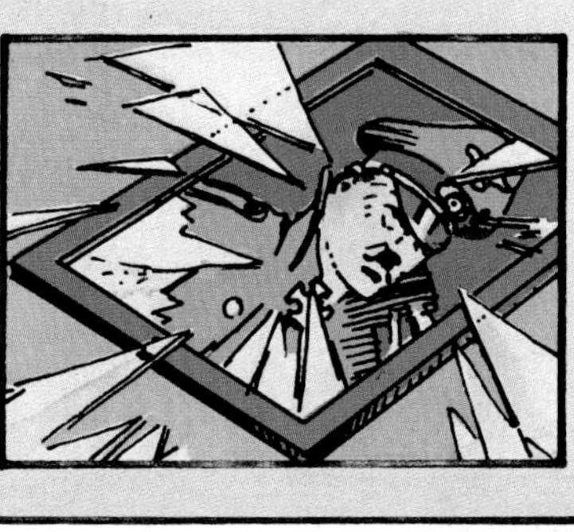

EPILOGUE

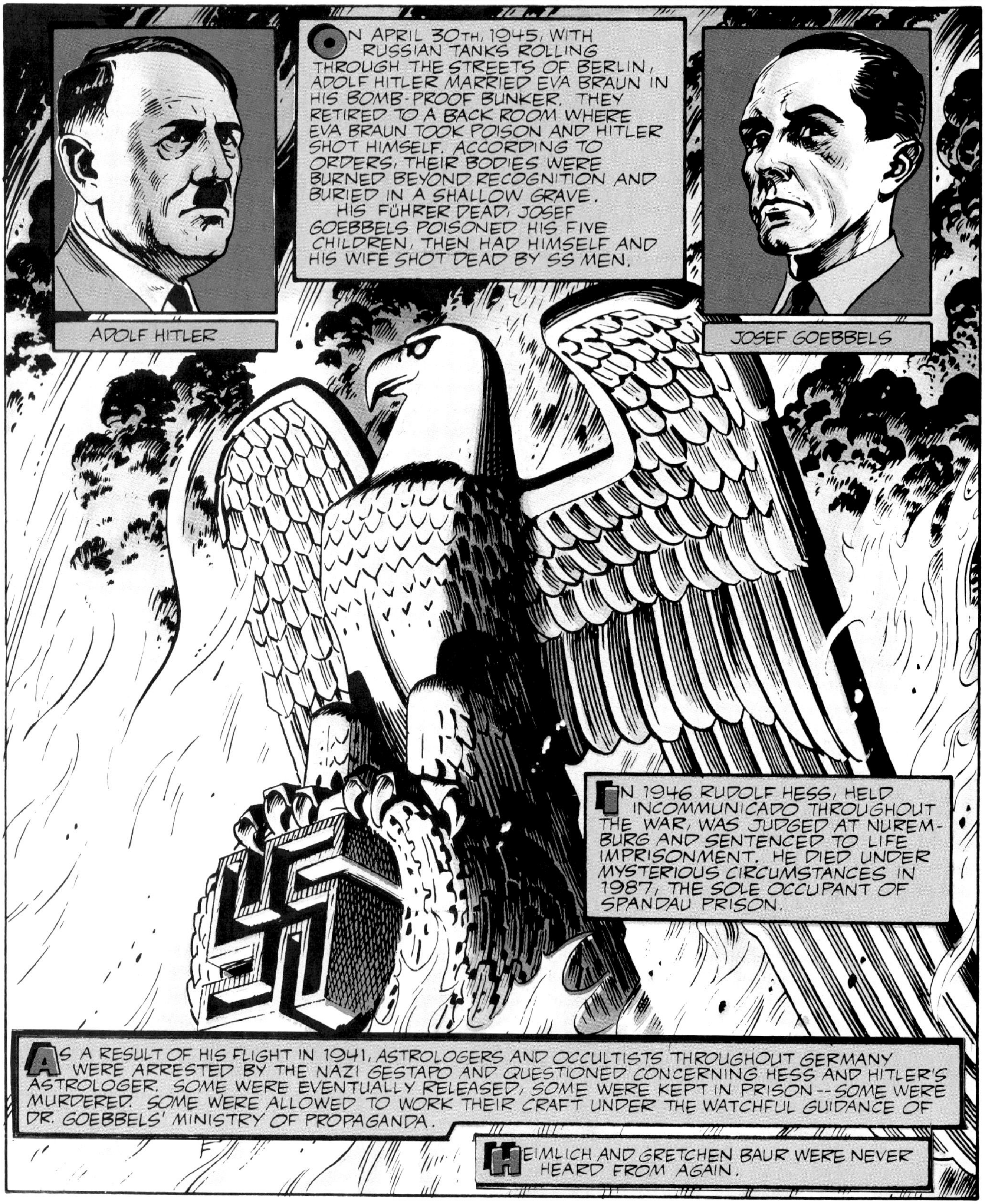
ON APRIL 30TH, 1945, WITH RUSSIAN TANKS ROLLING THROUGH THE STREETS OF BERLIN, ADOLF HITLER MARRIED EVA BRAUN IN HIS BOMB-PROOF BUNKER. THEY RETIRED TO A BACK ROOM WHERE EVA BRAUN TOOK POISON AND HITLER SHOT HIMSELF. ACCORDING TO ORDERS, THEIR BODIES WERE BURNED BEYOND RECOGNITION AND BURIED IN A SHALLOW GRAVE.
HIS FÜHRER DEAD, JOSEF GOEBBELS POISONED HIS FIVE CHILDREN, THEN HAD HIMSELF AND HIS WIFE SHOT DEAD BY SS MEN.
ADOLF HITLER
JOSEF GOEBBELS
IN 1946 RUDOLF HESS, HELD INCOMMUNICADO THROUGHOUT THE WAR, WAS JUDGED AT NUREMBURG AND SENTENCED TO LIFE IMPRISONMENT. HE DIED UNDER MYSTERIOUS CIRCUMSTANCES IN 1987, THE SOLE OCCUPANT OF SPANDAU PRISON.
AS A RESULT OF HIS FLIGHT IN 1941, ASTROLOGERS AND OCCULTISTS THROUGHOUT GERMANY WERE ARRESTED BY THE NAZI GESTAPO AND QUESTIONED CONCERNING HESS AND HITLER'S ASTROLOGER. SOME WERE EVENTUALLY RELEASED, SOME WERE KEPT IN PRISON -- SOME WERE MURDERED. SOME WERE ALLOWED TO WORK THEIR CRAFT UNDER THE WATCHFUL GUIDANCE OF DR. GOEBBELS' MINISTRY OF PROPAGANDA.
HEIMLICH AND GRETCHEN BAUR WERE NEVER HEARD FROM AGAIN.

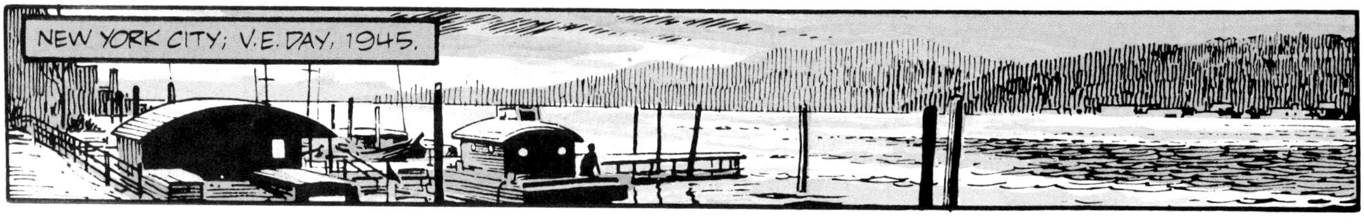
NEW YORK CITY; V.E. DAY, 1945.